Single Principles

Single

Principles

The Single Woman's Ten Step Guide to Power

Sheron C. **P**atterson

Library of Congress Catalog Card Number 93-9396

Second Edition

The scripture quotations in *Single Principles* are from the New Revised Standard Version of the Holy Bible

Inquiries should be addressed to
PERSEVERANCE PRESS
6212 Samuel Boulevard, Suite 148
Dallas, Texas 75226

Printed in U.S.A. by
Mission Communications
P.O. Box 222198
Dallas, Texas 75222
(214) 630-6495

To women

who are ashamed

of their singleness

This book could not have been written without the prayerful collaboration of many. I am indebted to the countless churches that invited me to preach, teach and counsel with their single adult ministries. A special thanks is in order to my editor, Garlinda Burton, for her relentless quest for perfection, and her devotion to this project. A cadre of friends also made this book possible. Althea Satterfield, Jennifer Wilder, Jackie Leonard, Cheryl Williams, Delphine Vassar-Bates, and Alyce Goff each read my manuscript and offered new ideas, as well as constructive criticism. I will always be grateful to my parents, William and Johnsie Covington, for the faith they continue to demonstrate in my ministry with single adults. Eternal thanks are due to my husband, Robert, who is not intimidated by this empowered woman of faith, and who encourages me to help other women toward their own empowerment.

Contents

Introduction

There are times in every single woman's life that she needs a boost of confidence. There are times when she needs to hear that she is O.K. just as she is. Even the most confident, happy, and well-adjusted single woman faces occasional self-doubt or a dip in self-esteem. This is a guidebook for you during those times.

This book offers straight talk about the challenge faced by Christian single women. Each chapter encourages you to use your faith in God to meet the challenges. Each principle illustrates how God can be brought more fully into your life.

Straight talk is something that you may not have heard from a Christian minister. For too long, the concerns of single women have been ignored or avoided by those of us charged with giving pastoral care to all people. With this book I will endeavor to open the dialogue about the challenges of being single in a "couples" culture.

The context of this book is here and now, and the foundation is biblical. Found within are the tools for your survival.

This book is a result of my ministerial calling to be a true pastoral caregiver to single adults. Since 1982 I've worked with men and women in singles ministries across the nation. It was the needs and concerns of single women, however, that commanded my attention and specialization. Women handle their singleness differently than men. Too often there is shame, disgust, panic, and desperation. I am convinced that these negatives are strongest when the woman's relationship with God is weakest. I want to help single women grow stronger by claiming God's power.

I realize that I am not super human, but I do want to transform the negative experiences of singleness for as many women as possible. Single women who place their lives securely into the hands of God are empowered. Their relationships with God give them strength, hope, faith, perseverance, joy, peace and grace. Thusly, they can handle any situation due to the power of God in them.

Each of the 10 Single Principles showcases the strength of empowered women, and examines reasons why more women are not empowered. The empowered women I've written about in each chapter illustrate the words of the angels, "With God, nothing will be impossible."

As you read the following pages I pray that you will allow the words to minister to you and lead you into an empowered existence.

Principle One

**Life without a husband
is a blessed life just the same.**

SINGLE WOMAN, YOU ARE SOMEBODY WONDERFUL ALL BY YOURSELF. You are O.K. just as you are. As a single woman you have power to be, to feel, and to become anything that you desire. Your power comes from God, and it is at your fingertips if you dare to use it. Search the Bible cover to cover. You won't find a single scriptural mandate that you must be married to enter heaven. These ideas do not exist in the Bible, but in the minds of an ill-informed majority culture.

Historically, status has been wrongly defined as a curse. Single women have always battled an ancient, omnipresent, oppressive force in society that seems determined to keep a woman without a man on the bottom of the barrel. Hundreds of single women have told me of their painful encounters with this oppressive force. Here is what they've endured.

After Mary's divorce, friends, family and colleagues told her that she "wasn't a whole person" because she did not have a husband.

After she separated from her husband, members of Jackie's church suggested that she resign as children's Sunday school teacher.

When Lula's husband died, her children suddenly felt that they had the right to dictate where their mother should mourn, how she should mourn, and when she should mourn.

Sheila dreads going to gatherings at her church because she knows that well-meaning members will ask the ubiquitous question, "Why aren't you married yet?"

This book seeks to help you hear a positive, hopeful voice among the negative. This book wants to remove the sting from your singleness. It is based on the lives of numerous powerful single women who've demonstrated that being manless does not mean being powerless. These women illustrate that for a single woman to be happy and whole, she must first learn to find happiness within herself.

This book also suggests steps for redefining relationships with men. Empowered single women know that such relationships are a choice. Single women have the God-given right to make such decisions. Most of all, the ideas explored here are based on the Bible, and the conviction that when you are in charge of your life, and happy with yourself, you are pleasing God.

Confronting the real world

Admit it. We live in a world where every creature that is considered normal seems to come in pairs. Even the animals of Noah's ark were gathered two by two. Living life solo seems awkward and off balance. Television and movies reinforce the notion that happiness is a husband who comes home to you after a hard day at the office. If you have a candlelight dinner on the table for him, all is well with the world.

Popular music also reinforces the message that a loving relationship with a man is what a woman needs to make her whole. Consider the musical message: "He makes my world come alive." "I revolve around his love." "Without him I am nothing." Translation, if I don't have a man in my life why bother even getting up in the morning?

In biblical stories, especially in the Old Testament, manless women were considered worthless women in every conceivable way. Legally they could not protect, feed, shelter, or support themselves. In those days every woman of merit was married off as early as puberty. Unmarried women were assumed to be mentally abnormal, physically unhealthy, or deformed. They were pitied and cast out. As with many women today, those who never married were labeled, despised or pitied.

Beginning with Genesis, a woman's worth has been determined by her proximity to a man. Genesis 2:18 says that "it is not good for man (or a woman, especially) to be alone." Over the years that quotation has been cast as a mallet, and used to knock single women. Each repetition of the Genesis passage seems to say "if you don't have a man, you are not worth squat!"

The manless and the powerless

Widows, Naomi and Ruth are two Old Testament women of the faith, whose story painfully illustrates the trials that women faced in those days, if they found themselves without men.

As the book of Ruth begins, Elimelech, Naomi's husband, has just died. Soon after, their two married sons Mahlon and Chilion also die. Three formerly married women who once had stature and standing in the community through their husbands, are now left alone. With the deaths of their spouses comes the deaths of the women's "somebodiness." When the widows realize their new uncertain status, their fear almost overwhelms them.

Mother-in-law Naomi tells the two younger women that she is powerless to aid them. "I have no other sons in my womb for you,"

Naomi said. (Barrenness of the womb was also considered a curse on Old Testament womanhood.) "And if I did they'd be too young for you now." She urges her daughters-in-law to return to their respective homelands, find new husbands and begin to live again through new men. Daughter-in-law Orpah accepts this sage advice, probably taking the first camel back home.

Ruth chooses to stay with Naomi. She underscores her devotion to Naomi with one of the most beautiful recitations on women's friendships, love and loyalty ever recorded. Ruth's words are a pledge of support and love to Naomi. These words found in Ruth 1: 16-17, offer a glimpse of her power to determine her own future.

"Entreat me not to leave you," Ruth says. "Or to return from following you. For where you go I will go, and where you lodge I will lodge; your people shall be my people, and your God, my God, where you die, I will die and there I will be buried."

There was so much power in that speech. There was even potential power in her manless status. Ruth had within herself the ability to carve out a personhood based on who she was. The bond of sisterhood established between Ruth and Naomi was an unstoppable source of power. Anytime women can unite around common sorrows and triumphs we form alliances that enable us to overcome. As support teams for each other we can soothe the sting of singleness, move forward, and press on. We need to form such alliances.

Do you feel stranded at the crossroads in your life? Has your husband just died? Are you divorced, or never married? Uniting with other women can be a major means of survival and sanity. Organize and plan women's support groups, weekly lunch or dinner gatherings, prayer groups or Bible studies. When we come together we see that we are not alone and that the challenges we face are not unique or "abnormal."

You can probably guess how I would have liked the Naomi and Ruth adventure to end: two strong women of faith walk off into the sunset, confident that they can make it as a duo.

Ruth and Naomi do use their bond to better their lot, but within the boundaries of what is acceptable in a male-dominated society. They work together to find a husband for Ruth with enough wealth to support Naomi too.

Separating the fairy tale from faith

I'm glad Ruth found her prince, and I would like, in a perfect world, for all women to be involved in healthy, mutually supportive, loving relationships with men, if they chose. But the significant moral of the Ruth and Naomi story is that the Lord will make a way somehow. The real good news is that faith and mutual support among women can equal a happy, productive life, whether one is single or married. With faith, any number of happy endings are possible. With fairy tales, the only happily ever after for women is with men as husbands.

Blending faith with fairy tales begins in our childhood. Our earliest recollections of God as taught in many Sunday schools is of God, the great omnipotent, divine matchmaker and do-gooder. And if you're a good girl, God will pair you up with a good Christian man. Along with our daily bread and deliverance from evil, we fairy-tale Christian women expect that God will send a loving male partner to take care of us.

As girls we are trained to anticipate the arrival of "Mr. Right." I personally can attest to 10 years of piano lessons from Mrs. Oliver, 10 years of dance lessons from Mrs. Young, and a host of cultural experiences heaped upon me all in the name of preparing me for the perfect mate. Having to practice piano on the sunny afternoons while the neighborhood boys played outside seemed highly unfair to me back then. What were the boys doing to prepare for Miss Right? I wondered. Mature Christians know the difference between faith and fairy tales. Faith in God—not romance— is fuel for your life's journey. Faith propels you through tough times. Faith gives you the ability to navigate through darkness by Christian will and not sight. True faith is the utmost confidence that God is with you every step of the way in life, whether you are single or married.

Conversely, fairy tales are made-up stories with pat, sappy endings. In fairy tales everything and everybody always are wonderful. Fairy tales make you wait in vain for the knight in shining armor to make your life complete and beautiful.

As a woman of faith you should know that happiness, peace and well-being don't come from an external source. Fulfillment and power come by recognizing that Almighty God is with you now.

Christianity and your reality

Of course, with all of society's messages and indoctrinations, it is easy to understand why so many of us cling to the fairy tale. It does not seem right somehow to be without a man. It goes against our "programming" as a woman.

That's the way my friend Carol, explained it over lunch one day. "The God I serve has got to have someone out there for me," said the 37-year old, polished investment banker.

I knew what I needed to say to Carol. As her pastor and friend, I told her what I've told so many others.

"Let's try a strong dose of reality. Carol, there are very few full-time knights in shinning armor available," I told her. "That means good men (Christian, employed or employable, self-respecting, woman-respecting, drug-free and nonviolent), are hard to find.

Those few "knights" are out-numbered by men, who for whatever reason oppress, undervalue, and malign strong, self-loving women.

"I have no way of predicting whether or not you'll find the man of your dreams, but I am convinced that you need God beside you to pick you up when you fall, to love you when you feel unloved, and to bless you when you feel unworthy."

I want you to have a man but...

I took my frank discussion with Carol one step further. "I want you to have a man," I said. " But not because everyone else has one, or because you feel left out, or its Christmas or your birthday and you want a special gift from someone special, or you can't stand being by yourself."

I celebrate my sisters who find healthy relationships with men. But I flatly object to the notion of having a man just because you think it's the thing to do.

I meet many women who carry themselves like Dorothy in "The Wizard of Oz." They spend a lot of precious time and energy searching for their heart's desire, (read: men), only to discover that what they long for has been inside them all the while.

Single woman, God loves you just as you are. That's the bottom line. God loves you whether you have a man or you don't, whether you date regularly or even if you haven't even been within breathing distance of a man for years. No connection exists between the intensity of God's love for you and the quality of your "love life." So, are you single? You are loved by the most important Being in the universe — God.

What's ahead

The second Principle is about developing self-esteem in single women. Empowered single women understand that they are lovable because Jesus said so. When this is the foundation for living, they can weather any of life's emotional storms. Once the water-gathering Samaritan woman in the book of John accepted Jesus' love, she became a new entity. Without self-esteem single women can't live the life that Christ wants for them.

The third, fourth, and fifth Principles will deal with Christian single women from three categories: always single, divorced, and widowed. Each type presents its own unique challenges. You can struggle and achieve along with the women in my case studies in their quest for power over their lives.

Principle six addresses single mothers and power. Empowered single mothers keep God in the center of their families and are blessed. Currently, 60 percent of families with children are headed by single parents, most of whom are women. Contrary to conservative naysayers, single mothers are not the curse of the stable family structure. Despite the difficulties, single parent families can foster personal fulfillment, hope and joy for children and adults.

Principle seven gives an overview of men from the perspective of empowered women. These women demonstrate that an iron-firm self-esteem is needed in order to interact successfully with men. Even in our male dominated society, single women have the power to define how they want to interact with the men in their churches, homes and in relationships.

How does the Christian woman of the '90s date? Principle eight presents the power of prayer as the primary ingredient for dating success. This chapter also reveals the possible pitfalls for women who attempt to date without a Christian foundation.

You are a sexual being. You are also a woman with choices. Well, what are you as a single Christian supposed to do about it? Society has one answer. The Lord has another. Empowered single women examine each choice and make a decision based on faith. In Principle nine, we will discuss one way Christians can make responsible, faithful decisions about sex.

The final Principle proclaims the reality that empowerment is an obligation. As single women become empowered they have a responsibility to pass it on to those who still dwell in spiritual and emotional confusion. This last chapter combines all you've learned in Principles one though nine, and suggests ways to use this power to make our world a saner place for single Christian women. Through Principle ten you'll consider empowerment ideas for possible programs and activities with your circle of friends, support group, club, church or religious community.

Each chapter ends with questions for personal reflection, an exercise intended to move you toward further empowerment and prayer.

Questions

1. What are other fairy tales Christian women tend to hold on to?
2. What other conclusions you can envision for the Ruth and Naomi story?

Exercise

List 25 ways God has allowed you to be powerful.

Prayer

Pray this prayer as you begin each chapter of this book.

Dear God,
Hallelujah, I am O.K. just as I am!
Awaken me to all the possibilities I possess through You.
Help me believe that my singleness is not a curse, but can be a blessing.
Open me to the possibility of change.
Let me read this book with sincerity.
Well up within me Your power source.
Never let me go.
Amen.

Principle Two

Love yourself first.

You've been had. Duped. Flim-flammed. Bamboozled. And hoodwinked. You've always believed that if you chased men and showered them with love, that you'd feel good inside. You've been taught that the only way to increase your self-esteem is by having a man in your life.

Well, those were lies. It is time to confront the truth.

Men are nice, but if you want to be happy, you'd better love yourself first. A primary love of self is the most noteworthy characteristic of the empowered Christian single woman. Healthy self- love is evident in women's concerns for themselves, and in the way women protect their human rights and personhood.

I've observed that empowered single women possess the strength to love themselves no matter what their circumstances are. They develop the ability to nurture the best of who they are, regardless of obstacles. They don't play second fiddle in any relationship. They know they count. They know they matter. They know God has given them a purpose in their lives. This is what makes them powerful.

Keeping love and concern for self prominent is hard work, but it's worth the effort. Consider the alternative: dependency and weakness. A woman who cannot love herself outside her intimate relationships will likely wind up making her needs the lowest priority in those relationships.

Simply put, self-love is a skill seldom taught to girls in Sunday school or home economics classes. Self-love helps you set boundaries on what you will and will not accept from other people. It raises your expectations; it determines how you carry yourself. It controls, to a significant degree, the actions of those around you, particularly the significant men in your life.

Pam: Get me to the well

The sun's fierce heat seemed to dare anyone with good sense to leave the shade. But Pam knew she had to go now to the town square's well for water, because not a drop was left in the house. Pam had chores that could not be done without water. Dishes, clothes, and children needed to be washed. Food begged to be cooked.

As a single mother, Pam had a seemingly unending burden. "It wouldn't be so tough," she thought, "if he'd lift a finger to help me around the house." He was Pam's latest live-in beau. She hoped they would marry soon. Despite her string of busted-up romances, Pam still believed that marriage could turn her dysfunctional lifestyle into paradise.

Deep inside Pam knew that if she made a wrong move with this new guy, like asking him to collect the water, that she might be left manless again. Pam swore that she's never let that happen. Five failed marriages was hard enough to explain. "Surely there is something wrong with me. Maybe this time I can get it right," she thought. "I'll keep quiet and do what I am told."

She knew it was better to wait until the sunset to venture to the well. Not so much hustle and bustle then. In the cool of the evening, the villagers generally relaxed, savoring the fruits of their day's work. But Pam decided not to put off her journey to the well. She took a deep breath, covered her head with a cloth for shade, and darted down the path toward the well.

You may know the rest of this biblical story found in John 4: 7-26. "Pamela"- the name I've given to the Samaritan woman at the well- reached her destination, and had the life-changing meeting with Jesus Christ. A thirsty Jesus got the water he needed, and a spiritually thirsty Pam got the water that she needed, too. Their encounter provides an excellent study of self-love and the single woman of faith. Pam was one of those single women who found it difficult to accept God's offer of unconditional love and acceptance. Heavy self-doubt seemed to whisper, "I am not worthy of you, your love, self-love or anybody else's love. I am the problem and I am beyond saving."

Pam's low self-esteem may have been due to her environment. We can see this first in her pattern of multiple marriages. Women, in Jesus' earthly era, had no rights, voice or power within the marriage relationship. Husbands had the right to at any time, end the marriage, for any reason, from sexual dissatisfaction, to bad cooking or a woman's so-called surly attitude.

To have been divorced five times indicates that Pam had repeatedly been a victim of the anti-single woman myths of her culture. She may have been living out a self-fulfilling prophecy of poor self-concept and failure. Pam's current relationship was another disaster waiting to happen. Living with someone or even relating to a man without benefit of marriage was considered a major religious violation in Pam's society. She risked it all just to "have" somebody. This is a vivid indicator of her desperation and low self-esteem.

Myths that haunt single women

Misinterpreted Christian doctrine can negatively impact a woman's self-esteem. Myths about what is acceptable or unacceptable Christian behavior continue to haunt women. Beverly and Gina are two women I know who suffered because they believed the myths.

"My faith demands that I accept whatever happens as God's will," said Gina, a 24-year old graduate student. By the time I met her, she had come to believe that constant suffering was a way of life for Christians. When the men she dated mistreated her, when her friends took her for granted, Gina merely shrugged her shoulders and said, "We Christians have our crosses to bear."

Gina misinterpreted the admonitions of Christian patience as meaning that Christian women were to be docile, pliable, and silent in the face of adversity. The more she suffered, the more she felt she was adhering to her faith. Gina had to learn the difference between suffering for Christ's sake and being victimized.

As a 40-year-old, always-single parent, Beverly felt like a serf to the men in her life. She felt excluded from power, even in her personal relationships. If God had wanted women to have control, it would have been spelled out in the Bible, she reasoned. As a woman, she was put on earth to comfort and pacify men.

I will never forget meeting Beverly while we were in seminary. Our first conversation went something like this:

"Hi, I'm Sheron. Which degree program are you in?"

Beverly responded, "I haven't decided yet. I'm looking for the one most geared to preparing women to support their men. I am here to serve man."

The ways the church has traditionally described God has shaped us into who we are as God's people. Gender-exclusive language in hymns and prayers presents God as a male and speaks of "man" inheriting the earth. But what of women? To Beverly, the Bible taught that men were ordained to be in control; therefore, she assumed her role to be subservient to men. Beverly had to learn that women and men are equals in the sight of God.

Byproducts of low self-esteem

Self-hate and self-doubt are two of the most lethal byproducts of low self-esteem evident among many single women of faith. But think; to doubt yourself is to doubt the God who created you and to doubt what God can do through you. To hate yourself is to hate one of God's creatures and to practice poor stewardship with yourself.

Pat and Jesse are single women who illustrate the destructiveness of self-hate and self-doubt.

Self-doubt fueled Pat's inability to make decisions about her future. Recently divorced, the 39-year-old dentist had dated her former husband ever since the 10th grade, and they'd married at the age of 18. When their marriage ended some 20 years later, Pat felt pressured to plunge immediately into the dating frenzy.

She jumped in too soon. Her first dating experience was a disaster. The broken marriage had battered her self-esteem. She felt responsible for the divorce and carried that blame and self-doubt into succeeding relationships. Inevitably, she attracted a man who seemed to have a radar for women with a stunted sense of self-worth, because he, too, lacked self-esteem.

He first spotted Pat from his perch in their church's choir stand, and he somehow knew she'd allow herself to be victimized. On their first dates he brought her candy and flowers. Then, after she was hooked on him, he began to take pleasure in seeing how much abuse she'd tolerate. He frequently made dates with Pat, then neglected to show up or even call. This continued for months because Pat was sure it was her fault. She'd ask herself over and over "What did I do wrong? What did I do to cause him to act this way?"

Pat and I talked in my office one morning about the situation. "Maybe I should just call him and ask why the relationship ended? It must have been something I said," Pat ventured. "I know if I could get him to talk to me, he would be able to pinpoint what I did wrong."

By this time, the man's "mind games" had paralyzed Pat. She believed that everything wrong in their relationship was her fault. Her story illustrates that, left unchallenged, self-doubt will make a fool out of you.

Jessie: A sister with an attitude

Jessie's self-hatred resonated in her voice. It growled and lashed out menacingly at passersby. From a mile away you could see that she was literally stewing in it. Jessie's self-hate showed in the very way she walked. The 52-year-old church librarian came stiff and cautious into a room, always anticipating trouble. You had the feeling she was just waiting for anyone to look at her half-way wrong.

Her divorce had been expected. "I never felt like I was a success at anything," she admitted one day. "All my life, my parents and siblings made me feel like I was the least and the lowest."

The criticisms from Jessie's childhood had become, loud, internal audio tapes, that played over and over again in her head.

Jessie felt bad about herself; those feelings in turn radiated outward. People avoided her, gossiped about her, and disliked her. Deep down she longed for close friends and a satisfying intimate relationship with a man, but the raging self-hatred stood like an impenetrable wall around her.

Anger became her only weapon. Rage became a means of elevating herself. Having a negative reputation was better than being ignored. She soon earned a reputation as a "sister with an attitude." She quarreled with members of her church, planted malicious gossip, undermined church programs and generally relished disrupting things. While some experts consider anger a valid, empowering emotion. Jessie's anger paralyzed her. If only she could release the self-hatred and allow the Lord to love her so she can begin to love herself and others.

Look through the eyes of the Savior

If you're trapped by a deflated sense of your own worth, try looking at yourself through the eyes of the Savior who has a genuine ability to appreciate and value women. Look at yourself through Jesus' eyes. Jesus wants everyone to love themselves as he loves them. His life-changing gospel was good news for self-esteem.

Read these words, reflecting for 20 seconds after each passage.

"Come unto Me, all who are heavy-laden and I will give you rest." (Matthew 11:28)

"I am the light of the world; those who follow Me shall not walk in darkness, but shall have light." (John 8:12)

"Peace I leave with you; My peace I give to you; not s the world gives, do I give to you. Let not your heart be troubled, nor let it be fearful." (John 14:1)

More and more single women are waking up to the reality that loving others first is a big mistake. Rather, they initially ensure that a love of self is in place and functioning well. The women presented in this chapter struggle with societal and biblical myths that hinder their ability to truly love and take care of themselves. In all such situations, the words and actions of Jesus are affirming and empowering. His power is your power.

Questions

1. Why do you think some women chose suffering rather than self-love?
2. What is the connection between angry women and self-hate?

Exercise

List 10 reasons why God loves you, citing Bible passages, if you choose. Make a list of the reasons why you love yourself.

Prayer

Pray this prayer every morning when you wake up for 7 days.

Dear God,
Open my eyes to the reality that self-love is not a sin.
Protect me from self-hate and self-doubt.
I want to feel good about myself.
I want life to be pleasant and free from concerns about who I'll be with tomorrow, or who will call tonight.
I want to be a woman who is confident in You.
Help me to see myself through Your eyes.
Amen.

1. God has given me his word that teaches, corrects & rebukes & trains in righteousness 2 Tim 3:16
2. I am fearfully & wonderfully made Psalms 139:14
3. I am God's child 1st John 3:1
4. God has given me the fruits of the spirit - love, joy, peace, patience kindness goodness faithfulness, gentleness & self-control! Gal 5:22
5. I am a light upon a hill that shines for all to see. Mat 5:14-16
6. God has given me the gifts of serving/encouraging Romans 12:7

Principle Three

**Always-single women,
this is your life.
Live it.**

7. I humble myself under God's mighty hand
1 Peter 5: 6,7

8.

MAYBE YOUR KNIGHT IN SHINING ARMOUR IS STUCK IN TRAFFIC. YOU might not meet him this week, this month, or 15 years from now. You have two choices. You can put your life on hold and wait, or you can accept God's choice for you to live fully and now.

I vote for mashing life's accelerator. Go for it.

The empowered single women that I've met also believe that a life that is not lived to the fullest is wasted. Period. They choose life instead of stagnation. But this choice requires courage and faith. Here's how one woman put her life in motion.

It was one of those rare, cool summer days in Dallas when our group of 15 buddies attended a baby shower for a friend's just-adopted child. Inside the house Carrie, a 2-year-old lightning rod prowled around the living room floor filled with gifts. Proud momma Kimberly was bragging that she'd gained the joys of motherhood without morning sickness, weight gain or episiotomy.

We were happy for her, but some of us could not help but wonder, "What's wrong with this picture?" Did the adoption mean that Kimberly had given up on marriage? Was she incapable of finding a husband? Should she have waited a little longer?

Kim, 32, is a no-nonsense woman. Like the rest of us she had always dreamed of meeting Mr. Right. Through college and development of her career, however, a suitable man had not materialized. She had dated lots of guys, but nothing long-term surfaced. By the time she reached her late 20s she began to panic at the idea of being 30 without a husband or children.

"I had to be strategic," Kim said matter-of-factly. "I knew I wanted to be a mother, and I knew I'd achieve it one way or the other. I've not thrown out the idea of getting married someday. But the idea of putting my other life plans on hold until I marry was unthinkable," she explained.

She had everything *but* the man

Kimberly and Carrie opened the gifts, I found myself assessing Kim's life. She had everything *but* the man: the house, the car, the career, now the baby. I could feel some other friends thinking, "Maybe I'll be forced to do this same thing in 10 years," or "Are the chances really that bleak that she had to get a baby on her own?"

We all pondered what the adoption meant to us. Kim's actions made us think about our own lives, and made us realize that we also are entitled to dream dreams of a house, a baby, a husband. The good news is, you can get *some* of them.

The challenge for always-single Christian women, as well as all single Christian women, is reaching their life goals within the framework of their faith. This framework is based on the words from the Jesus Christ. In Matthew 6:24 Jesus states, "No one can serve two masters, for either she will hate the one and love the other, or she will hold to one and despise the other. You cannot serve God and mammon."

Society offers many confusing messages concerning right and wrong. Use your faith to make decisions that are compatible with the scriptures. Motherhood via adoption makes incredibly good sense for always-single women who want to parent children.

Kim's actions demonstrate an ability to channel God's power to reach healthy life goals. Fortunately, she did not put her plans on hold, just because she couldn't have children the "traditional" way. Sadly, many churchgoers still bristle at the idea of a single woman enjoying a full life without a husband. They feel the woman is somehow cheating at the game of life; that children are trophies earned only after a woman puts on a long white gown, marches down a church aisle, and says "I do." But Jesus said in John 10:10, "I have come that they may have life and have it more abundantly." There is no mention of a mate as a requirement for receiving what Jesus has to offer.

The "Kims" of the world are blazing a new trail to happiness. They will multiply with our support, understanding, and applause. They demonstrate one way of seizing the power to love themselves and take care of themselves.

Murphy Brown and Christian choices

Murphy Brown is more than just a fictitious, single TV news anchor who gets pregnant and decides to keep the baby. The character, portrayed by actor Candice Bergen, represents a growing number of single women who purposely become pregnant and raise children with little thought to the implications of their professed faith. They figure if they can produce the baby, pay for it, and take care of it. "Why wait?" These women are tired of boyfriends' broken promises and their own frustrated dreams of a "normal" nuclear family. Some even select the babies' fathers like laboratory rats, weighing the men's abilities to shape the babies' intellect, and physique, rather than considering the men's potential as participatory fathers and husbands. As a pastor and a woman, I can understand and affirm the motives for many single women who give birth without being married. I wish that all women who want to be mothers could reach their goal. Yet I can't in good conscience advocate the "Murphy Brown" route to motherhood. In the framework of our Christian faith out-of-wedlock pregnancy fits like a square peg in a round hole.

Looking back on the Holy Spirit-inspired conception of Jesus, Matthew 1: 19-20 offers a glimpse of what the consequences were for women who found themselves pregnant and not married. Once Joseph discovered his fiancee' Mary was "with child," he planned to quietly end their relationship. Had her pregnancy been human in conception, the then unmarried Mary and her lover would have been in "trouble," because they had broken the Jewish laws dictating that men and women should first marry before they become sexually intimate. Similarly, Jesus frowned upon sex outside marriage. He condemned this act, known as fornication, in Mark 7:21.

Recipe for obsession

Some single women are wrestling with desperation, as it tries to push them into negative circumstances. For example, the pressure from parents on a single woman to "tie the knot" can spin her around like a tornado, dampen her spirits like a monsoon, and blow her over like a hurricane. The result is a beleaguered woman who'll do anything to get the family off of her back.

Soceity's obsessions with pushing single women to marry stems in part from the differences between the ways that boys and girls are reared and socialized. Women are conditioned to seek power and approval outside ourselves, and to devalue the power and legitimacy of self-love and self-respect that we are born with. In other words, women often are encouraged to look to someone else to make us happy. We are programmed from the cradle to yearn for male companionship in order to exist.

As a result, some obsessed women find themselves literally praying, "Now I lay me down to sleep, I pray the Lord, my soul to keep. If I should die before I wake, I pray the Lord, my soul will take. P.S. God, please don't forget my standing request for the man of my dreams.

Make him tall, dark and handsome, employed and a man who loves you as much as I do. And Lord, I'll try to be patient, but make this happen before I get too old! Amen."

Many single women feel this prayer is the appropriate petition to God, who is the giver of "every good and perfect gift." Like the child who knows that mom and dad will buy birthday presents, many single women look to God to dole out husbands and boyfriends like candy.

Soceity's pre-occupation with marriage often intensifies within some women as they age. Sybil, a woman I know, prayed to God for a man for three decades. When she reached 40, she could no longer keep her grievance with God to herself. As one of God's ministers, I became her complaint department.

"Why is God punishing me like this?" she asked me as tears rolled down her face one Sunday. Sybil felt God had betrayed her. She had done all the right things. She worshiped and praised God, read the scriptures daily, tithed at her church, attended Bible study, and even volunteered as a church usher. Didn't God realize that she was one of the faithful? Why had God turned a deaf ear to her prayers?

For many faithful Christian woman, it is downright embarrassing to be denied the desires of your heart. What about all the scriptures in the Bible that promise, "Ask in the name of Jesus and it shall be given?"

Sorry Sybil, no scripture in the Bible promises that a man will be provided for every woman. The only promised relationship is that Jesus will be by your side.

Alyson: Only make-believe

If there is no man in sight, some sisters like Alyson create one in their minds.

Alyson, 29, was very active in her church. Whenever her women friends talked about men, she dominated the conversation with anecdotes about her many dates. She talked at length about a broken engagement and the huge diamond ring she "threw back in his face."

The tragedy was not the busted romance, but that Alyson had been reduced to lying to her friends.

Alyson proudly cornered me after service one Sunday and described the latest fantastic man she was dating. In great detail she bragged about how much he loved her, the presents he bought her, and what he was going to do for her in the future.

But when I said, "Where is he? I'd like to meet him," her proud bearing dissipated. She stammered, "he is out of town a lot. He does not like large groups," and hurried away.

I discovered Alyson's boyfriends were imaginary during a conversation with her mother. Her mother explained that Alyson is embaressed by her singlehood. She believes that everyone has someone, except her. Rather than face condemnation by her peers for not having someone, Alyson does her best to fit in by pretending.

In actuality, the truth could produce a greater bond of sisterhood for Alyson and her friends. It may also stop some of her women friends from falsely embellishing their romantic lives, and move the group toward conversation topics that uplift them all.

Marion: Dateless and dorky

Marion had been dateless for years. It had become "a way of life for her," she bitterly pointed out.

"As a single parent if you don't have someone, you feel 'dorky.' You feel like everybody is laughing at you behind your back," she said.

Marion was a part of a singles group for which I conducted a retreat on self-esteem. I had asked each person in the group to list obvious traits of a person who lacked self-esteem. They quickly threw a verbal barrage of descriptions at me, and I wrote them on a chalkboard.

I first noticed Marion nodding her head vigorously at each adjective. "They were calling my name each time," she later told me. "I was unhappy as a single. I felt I had to get to get married. My unhappiness led to an eating disorder. I expressed my dissatisfaction with my singleness by eating and getting fat. Many a time I prayed I would die."

With God's help, Marion said, she was able to control her craving for food and for marriage. "I checked myself into a hospital. Things had gotten that bad. It was the best thing that I could have done for myself and my child," she continued.

"The counselors helped me to accept myself as I am. I learned how to stop waiting for my life to get better. I know that I am able, through Jesus' power, to make my life wonderful," Marion said.

Face the fear

If you stop running from the fear of singleness, and face it squarely, you can overcome that fear. Remember the story of David and Goliath? David whipped the giant, not by strength, but by fearlessness. God replaced David's fear with strength and bravery.

Speaking of strength and bravery, I conduct a workshop called "Will I Ever Marry?" I decorate the workshop room as if I'm hosting a wedding reception, with balloons, streamers and "Just Married" signs everywhere. Once the participants are seated I inform them that under one of their chairs is the bride's bouquet. The one who finds it is asked to stand and respond after I offer the following monologue: "Cathy was such a beautiful bride, and her new husband is fine! We should all be so lucky. Hey isn't that Susan and Jack over there? I hear they're getting married in two months. Camille is here with Jonathan. He's put a rock on her finger. I'm surprised that Page is here with Ken. I thought she was dating Darren, or was it Peter? Oh, the choices some of us have."

The women in the workshop are asked to respond with their own feelings. Usually, they use words like "lonely," "alienated," and "jealous" to describe how they feel. Some always-single women, see other women's marriages as juicy apples that dangle just out of their reach. The thought of never marrying conjures up stifling fear for many people, especially for single women over 30.

Facing the fear means answering some tough questions about your future. Imagine what your life will be like in 10 years, if you remain single. Imagine yourself 20 years from now and single. Confront the anxiety this image may bring. You may get married soon, or you may not. It's important to lay to rest those fears about singleness that hold you hostage, and prevent you from enjoying yourself today.

The Old Testament Psalms say much about overcoming fear and recognizing God's unstoppable power. Consider my liberal interpretation of Psalm 27:

"The Lord is my light and my salvation; whom shall I fear? The Lord is the defense of my life; whom shall I dread? Although loneliness and self-pity came upon me to destroy my self-esteem, they were not successful. Though depression and doubt encircle me, my heart will not fear. Though this world may not understand the peace I have within, I shall remain confident."

Active patience

Is there life without marriage?

Those best able to answer that are the relatively few women who have survived decades as always-single women. Some are nuns, "maiden aunts," retired teachers. Many are squirreled away quietly somewhere with the label "old maid" pinned to their old lace collars.

Joan refused to bow to those "old maid" stereotypes. We talked over coffee and desert one afternoon. I had known her for a few years professionally, but I'd never asked her about her life as an always-single women. She had such an air of well-being and confidence, that I had often wondered if and how her singleness could ever have been a problem for her.

The 61-year-old bank executive seemed to have it all. Her singleness was not a problem. It was just the way things were. Like the moon and the stars.

Joan confessed that her upbringing had a lot to do with her being comfortable with being single. "My parents never pressured me to marry. That's why I feel so positive about it," she explained. "Mom was a single parent for a while when she and my dad split up for a few years. She showed me that you can make it as a single women. In the late 1930s, she worked as a clerk, and made $15.00 a week. The three of us- my mom, my brother and me- lived in a boarding house. It was tough, but we made it," Joan proudly recalled.

"When I was growing up, women were expected to get married in high school or college, or no later than one or two years after graduating. At first, I didn't mind that I was always a bridesmaid, but never a bride, because I assumed I'd marry," she said.

"I noticed when I was in my 20s, my singleness tended to bother my friends more than it did me. They would ask me, 'What do single women do?' I'd tell them that we buy groceries, plan meals, and do yard work like every body else.

"I understood their discomfort. Marriage was society's norm, so naturally one assumes that something was "wrong" with those persons who weren't married," she said.

"I've always felt like a whole person. I am self-directed and I feel lucky that I have more time than married women to give others. Women with their own nuclear families don't always have much time to nurture and interact with others."

I asked Joan if she ever prayed for a husband? She chuckled, "I feel very close to God but, no, I've never prayed to God to send me a man. Being single is a fact of my life. I did not set out to be single, and I don't say that I absolutely won't marry. But I can't wait around for a husband to help me live a full life."

Always-single woman, the ball is in your court. What are you going to do with it? Much is possible for you. Do not wait on anyone to do it for you. The always-single women in this chapter are in various stages of facing the fear of being alone. Dare to envision your future as a single woman. Whether this is your reality or not, know that if God is with you, you will never be alone.

Questions

1. Have you ever invented an imaginery boyfriend, and lied about it to your friends, co-workers or relatives?

2. What's the worst thing that can happen to you if you remain single?

Exercise

List 10 advantages to being single. Believe what you write.

Prayer

Pray this prayer before lunch for 7 days.

Dear God,
With you I am never alone.
Strengthen me to live a full life with the circumstances I have.
Enable me to face each day with freshness and zest.
Help me to find joy and purpose with my life.
You are my power source.
You are the energy I need to soar.
I want to be a frequent flyer.
Amen.

Principle Four

**Divorced women,
your marriage failed,
not God.**

TO HEAR SOME FOLKS TELL IT, DIVORCE IS THE WORST THING THAT CAN happen to a woman.

Many women also view divorce as a no-win solution to a deteriorating marriage and prayers that seem to go unanswered. As a result, divorcees' experience shame and spiritual confusion. They feel victimized by their faith, betrayed by God, and penalized because they chose to end their marriages.

The empowered divorced women I know understand that their marriages failed, but God did not. They live full lives because they believe God is with them, and they will survive. Here's how one woman conquered the difficulties of divorce.

Kay: One survivor's saga

I sat in Kay's cozy bungalow, celebrating with her, yet another survivor of divorce. Her home was small, but it seemed a palatial mansion to Kay, a 34-year-old secretary. She was grateful. Five years ago, when she left her ex-husband, Robert, she exited virtually empty-handed.

"I left the apartment with a sewing machine, a television, a typewriter, and my 6-year-old twin girls," said Kay, remembering the day she reluctantly walked out. "He kept the apartment, the car, and the major stuff because it was all in his name."

Kay's 10-year marriage ended after a turbulent drama acted out before the students and faculty of the law school Robert attended. A third-year student, Robert had fallen in love with Karen, a first-year student in 1983. As this very public affair blossomed, Kay felt like the eyes of the law school were upon them.

She had been reared in a strict, Bible-believing home, in which divorce was never an option. In her words, "Divorce reaped the worst damnation possible." As her marriage crumbled, she feared divorce. "I felt chained to a disaster that I did not create," she said.

"I never thought it would happen to me. I thought my faith was invincible, and would see us through. Robert and I were active in church, for nine years we prayed together," Kay emphasized. After the divorce Kay slowly moved from being a victim to being a survivor by understanding that she was not alone. She found comfort in the reality that God's love and forgiveness were available to her even in the midst of her divorce.

Divorce: What the Bible really says

Spiritually, the biggest hurdle for the Christian woman going through a divorce, is confronting what some mistakenly believe the Bible says about her. As was mentioned in Principle 1, the scriptures have sometimes been used by the ignorant and the misinformed as weapons to hurt and weaken women. There exists, in some circles a pervasive and erroneous belief that divorced Christians are not true Christians. The insinuations are, "If you really had faith you would pray together, stay together, and work the situation out. If you had the Christian commitment you would forgive."

In the Old Testament divorce was a device whereby a man could leave an unsatisfactory wife for whatever reason he chose. According to the laws of Moses, in Deuteronomy 24:1, a man could divorce a woman who simply "no longer found favor" in her his eyes. To enact the divorce, he had only to write, "I am no longer your husband. You are no longer my wife. He then put the document in her hand and banished her from his house.

To this day, many people treat a divorced woman as an outcast. But that was then; this is now. Divorce may mean a relationship has failed, but you are still a child of God. There is nothing wrong with you. Your marital love may have died, but God's love is eternal. You are divorced from your husband. But you can never be separated from God. Your "somebodiness" did not come from your husband. It comes from God and you still have it.

Persecution of divorced women also stems from some misinterpretations of Jesus' comments on this topic. In the New Testament passage Matthew 5:31, Jesus talks about divorce in no uncertain terms. In a conversation with a group of religious leaders, who already had a long running feud on the topic, Jesus said, "Everyone that divorces his wife, except for the cause of unchastity, makes her commit adultery; and whoever marries a divorced woman commits adultery."

From a 1990s vantage point, Jesus affirms the sanctity and holiness of marriage. Jesus forthrightly reinforces the conviction that marriage is not like a toy that amuses until our attention span needs something new. But Jesus understands that divorce happens due to human failure. None of us are perfect. In holding up marriage, Jesus is pointing to the ideal for which we should strive. Being a divorced woman does not end your life, your faith, or relationship with God.

The rest of this chapter focuses on divorced women who are in the process of leaving the pain and frustration of divorce behind them. They are in various stages of understanding divorce as a passing mistake, rather than an everlasting error.

Elaine: She lacked love

Elaine changed husbands the way a bad driver changes lanes on the freeway: often and for no apparent reason. With five divorces to her credit, she was eager to find husband number six.

She lacked the power to love and be content with herself. At first glance, you'd never notice the deficit. Elaine was considered a saint of her church. If a meal needed to be cooked, or a down-on-his luck member needed rent money or a ride to the grocery store, Elaine was always there.

Upon closer inspection, however, I learned that she maintained the at-your-service-stance, not because she enjoyed giving service but because serving others gave her a sense of worth. Elaine was what some psychotherapists call a "rescuer," someone so consumed by the needs of others that she could not focus on her shortcomings and needs. She had become incapable of forming lasting love relationships.

A first step toward empowerment for Elaine was learning how to be alone but happy. God gives us the strength to be alone. It sounds funny, doesn't it, developing the skill to be alone? But that skill is the difference between being alone and being lonely. This power is rooted in the conviction that God is always with you. As a team, you and God are invincible. Remember Psalm 23:4, "I will fear no evil, for thou art with me."

Rita: Wrong from the start

The phone seemed to jump off the hook when it rang at 3:00 a.m. Rita was calling. Though only a longtime friend would recognize her over the sobs and wails. Between high-pitched moans, she blurted, "He told me to get out of his house now!"

He was Leon, Rita's husband of three months, telling her that the marriage was over.

She calmed down a little and said, "I can't believe he's being so cruel. I feel like I don't even know him anymore."

Truer words were never spoken. Yes, Leon and Rita had pledged their love and commitment to each other before a congregation of witnesses at their church wedding: but they were strangers. Rita married him because she felt she needed to be married. She had always wanted to marry simply because everybody else was doing it, and she felt left out. Years before she met Leon, another beau had proposed to her but backed out after most of the wedding plans had been made. Coming that close without marrying had made Rita vulnerable. She jumped at the next proposal. Leon and Rita both were writers at the same newspaper. They had known each other professionally, but when a special project brought them into close association for a month, the sparks flew. After the first date Rita knew she was in love.

Leon was 10 years her senior, and seemed a caring, compassionate Christian man, who wanted her as much as she wanted him. In Rita's eyes age and church attendance were synonymous with responsibility and commitment. "Hey, he's active in his church. He teaches Sunday school class and ushers. How much more trustworthy can he be?" she asked.

Rita wanted to trust somebody. Women of faith commonly trust a lot, maybe too much. Maybe we always look for the good in men because we have faith that deep down inside, God makes everyone trustworthy.

Yes, God gives all persons the potential to be worthy of trust. The reality is that everyone does not accept God's gift due to the high requirements, namely, commitment, honesty and sincerity.

Rita trusted Leon so much that she ignored the warnings about the pitfalls of being a "loose" woman from her mother and Auntie Rose. Rita began an intense sexual relationship with Leon. For her, having sex meant offering all she had to Leon in hopes of holding on to him. Six months after the relationship began Rita became pregnant. She could not believe she had become an unmarried, pregnant, Christian woman.

"Those three words just could not fit into any sentence describing me," she recalled. "What could I say to my mother? How could I face my pastor?

Marriage, she decided, was the only way out of this mess. For his part, Leon too felt pressured to marry Rita. People at the office knew that he was dating her and they would naturally assume the baby was his. As her abdomen swelled, so did the pressure on Leon to propose. The wedding plans were made. Maternity wedding gowns are hard to find. Rita had her's custom made. She was determined to walk down the aisle in white.

It was just after the baby was three-months-old that the frantic late-night phone calls to me from Rita started. Leon had begun to release the stored-up resentment and anger inside himself. A few weeks later, Rita and the baby had moved out. Leon and Rita divorced by the end of the year.

Looking back on the five-month marriage, Rita now admits that the divorce should never have happened because the marriage should never have happened. "I married because I was lonely and pregnant." The responsibility and commitment that Rita saw in Leon was actually her own longing for wholeness. She assumed Leon could make her life whole.

But Rita learned the hard way that no one is responsible for her happiness but her.

Til abuse do we part

Empowered single women know if the marriage hurts, it hurts God too. "Til death do us part" is not a license for a husband to pound a wife into a near-death coma. There is a growing confidence among single women that God would rather aid the emotional healing after a broken relationship than to have women suffer broken bones, and remain in violent relationships.

In 1985, when I was a religion writer for a national Christian newspaper, I was prompted to write a series of articles on violence in the Christian home, after reading studies on domestic violence. The most startling statistic is that every 4 seconds a woman in America is beaten by somebody she loves. Also, I had been shocked to discover that more incidents of spousal abuse occur in "Christian" homes than in "non-Christian" homes. And the wife battering in homes of the Christians often resulted from a deadly combination of misinterpreted scriptures about "submission," and mental illness, drug or alcohol abuse and codependency.

Though prayer, meditation, and fasting can help an abused woman get more in touch with God, those things alone, will not make an abusive spouse stop beating, berating, and belittling her. Divorce may be the only way to save the life.

Michelle: The young and the reckless

In my work in singles ministry I've encountered battered women of many races and backgrounds. Like Michelle, each one dreaded the thought of ending the marriage in hopes that her husband would change, but most sought divorce as the only way to stop the beating.

By the time she was 18, Michelle had two children. Henry her husband spent most of his time in a drunken stupor. The family spent Friday nights at the local racing speedway. Each weekly outing culminated in a public fisticuffs and cursing exchange between Henry and Michelle.

They started dating in high school. Henry loved to race his hot rod through the rural lanes of their small town. Michelle loved Henry's dangerous, exhilarating personality. Soon after they married and their first child was born, Henry was seriously injured in a racing accident.

Michelle had been a passenger in the car at the time. "The car flipped over seven times," she recalled. "I walked away without a scratch.

"Henry sustained massive head injuries, however, and to this day has a metal plate in his head. "It seemed like I owed him something due to the crash. I felt I ought to stay because he needed me," she said.

Michelle's guilt was compounded by her memories of a childhood in the home of alcoholic parents. Her father had sexually molested her and her sisters while they were growing up, and Michelle's mother never intervened. The scars from home left Michelle with an extremely fragile self-esteem. She now admits that she probably would have left home with whomever came along.

"I was damaged goods, and I did not care what happened to me," she remembered. "The fast-paced life of Henry's professional racing gave me a feeling of running away from all the pain of childhood. But whenever we slowed down, the pain from my past caught up with me."

In his despair over his injuries, Henry increased his drinking. "The more he drank, the harder the blows were. Michelle thought that she could survive them by fighting back. "I believed back then, if I could submit to sex with my father, surely I could endure a few beatings," she said.

One day, though, Henry beat her so badly that she had to go to the hospital. The chaplains there knew her by name. One of them took Michelle to his office and asked, "Is this what God had in mind for your life?" she recalled.

"I realized that though I didn't know a lot about God, I knew that God wanted a better life for me. So I sat there and prayed for strength to pick myself up and move on."

At 28, Michelle suddenly realized her inner power. She finally understood that she did not deserve ill-treatment. She had learned eventually that God's love for her was greater than the personal and social pressure to stay married, no matter what.

Divorced women of faith demonstrate a deep commitment to God through their ability to love themselves enough to separate from negative relationships. They know that the end of a marriage is not the worst event in life. The worst thing that could happen is that shame and spiritual confusion cause them to lose their faith in God. The women in this chapter know the spiritual and societal sting of divorce, but they know the Lord has the power to heal their wounds and move them forward.

Questions

1. How do you handle societal and religious pressure toward divorce?
2. Are you a victim or survivor of divorce?

Exercise

Use a concordance to locate all the biblical passages about divorce. Read each one and develop your own understanding of what the Bible is really saying. Then read biblical passages about Jesus and his forgiveness, and realize that your sins are forgiven.

Prayer

Pray this prayer before you go to bed at night for 7 days.

Dear God,
My loss was great, but You are greater.
I seek to move on from the past.
Today is a blessing from You.
Let me use it to Your glory.
I believe that You can accomplish great things in my life.
Guard me from the fears that surround me.
Erase yesterday's failures that continue to cling.
Bind up the wounds of brokenness I feel.
I can survive and even thrive if I do not lose faith.
Amen

Principle Five

Widowed women can find life after death.

MOURNING AND BEREAVEMENT ARE NOT MEANT TO BE ETERNAL FOR widowed women. Grief may knock you to your knees, but God picks you up, wipes away the tears, comforts your heartache, and then says, "Live in my Name!"

You have lost a husband, but God is not finished with you yet. Don't spend too much time feeling sorry for yourself—empower yourself. The empowered widows whom I've met tell me there are at least two good reasons why widows should choose power over self-pity: your husband is dead, not you; and God still has a purpose for your life.

Consider Rosa's story. Her tears were still fresh the day we sat on her front porch and talked. Her husband George, had died just ten days before. The memories of him first in the hospital bed, then in a coffin were still in her mind. She wanted to remember him, but she also knew that she had to get on with her new life alone.

At 71, Rosa is a quiet, strong woman, who has been active in church all her life. She has seen the power of God work many times in other folks' lives. After her husband's death, she needed God to work in her life.

"After the funeral, one of my married friends called to console me," Rosa recalled. "She told me, if her husband died before her, she'd simply go with him; she would never live alone."

That conversation was a turning point for Rosa. "I scolded her good," Rosa chuckled. "The truth is we all can go on with life. We do go on, if we stick with God.

"I do miss George. I cry for him," she admitted. "But I'm not totally destroyed due to his death because I know that God will lead me out of this trial and on towards another blessing."

Rosa is operating from the position of empowerment. Her husband is no longer living. She does not fantasize his return. She also understands that she is still living and that life goes on.

Not pity but power

Not all widows have reached this stage. Some are trapped in a "widow's rut," where they act out ancient roles foisted upon them. Many biblical images of widows are women who are needy and pitiful. The widowed woman in Deuteronomy 25:5-10 was expected to continue living with her husband's family after his death and, in effect, be passed on as wife to other brothers in descending order of age. 1

Timothy 5:1-16 details not only what widows should and should not do, but how church members are to treat them. Only the chaste, married-only once, and "God-centered" widow is said to deserve the church's support.

Above all else the widow was to be pathetic. One of the most heart-wrenching scenes comes from 1 Kings 17:3, when the prophet Elijah approached the widow of Zarephath and asked her for food. She was a kind and generous woman, who experienced life as a widow with tremendous hardship. This unnamed woman believed that she was destined to die of starvation, and she was preparing the last meal before she and her son died.

As a result of these limiting images of widows, it is understandable that today's widows follow those who've gone before them in powerlessness.

Take Mabel for example. She chose pity. Mabel reveled in her widowhood, and she enjoyed showing it off like a new pair of shoes. She was the classic unempowered widow—suffering, lonely, helpless. Her husband's death was the crutch she leaned on for survival. In reality, she was afraid of the new person she might become. Rather than accept who she is , Mabel lives in the past. Worst of all, she has no confidence in herself to make major decisions, so she asks other family members to run her life. She is powerless, weak, and vulnerable to abuses of all sorts.

It doesn't have to be like that anymore. Daughters of God, you deserve the best. You should not be chained to grim role models and boxed into a bleak predetermined future.

A widow with a "made up mind"

You can't stop a woman with a made up mind, as the saying goes. My favorite biblical widow illustrates this. She shed some tears, recovered, and then hustled to made a new life for herself. In Luke 18:1-8 we meet this widow, who was alone in the world, and who needed protection. She found out where she could get this protection and asked for it. The source of what she needed was an obstinate, godless judge, who refused to help.

This widow had a choice to make. She could have whimpered in a corner, and waited for her adversaries to devour her. But instead she rolled up her sleeves and worked for what she needed. She was relentless in demanding, protesting, hounding, and harassing the judge until she received the help she needed.

Like the widow-heroine of Luke 18:1-8, my friend Edna has a lot of guts. Edna shuns the term "widow" to describe herself, even though her husband died 15 years ago. She has not remarried.

" 'Widow' " has connotations I do not like," she told me once. "I hear it and I think, " 'O poor thing.' That does not describe me at all."

At 75, Edna has no intentions of sitting in a rocking chair and depending on someone else. She's active in civic groups, and in organizations within her church. She exudes a sense of somebodiness and she knows this is her key to success.

"I know I am blessed because I think differently than some other widows," Edna said. "I was somebody before I got married to him. Nothing or no one can take that away from me."

Widowhood was not always so easy for Edna. At first she grieved Jim's death terribly. The worse times came after all the attention from friends and the sympathetic phone calls stopped. Nights were the worst time. She could not sleep. "I was afraid to lay my head down," she said.

What made the difference was her determination to survive. "I have other friends who all but died when their husbands died," she said. "The loss of a spouse is truly a traumatic event, but life must go on."

Maya: Tried by the fire

Common to all widows is their understandable battle with grief. The good news as found in Psalm 30:5 is: "Weeping may endure for a night, but joy cometh in the morning." Here are two stories of women who found that joy.

Maya is a well-respected clergywoman, admired by many because she exudes power, a sense of direction and self-assurance. What many people don't know is that Maya was once a housewife who, incidentally, was timid as a mouse, and who lived for and through her husband. When he died, it was as if a fire had destroyed her whole world. But God has a way of refining and purifying us by life's fires. Maya was 30 when her husband died of cancer. Now, at 45, she can look back and measure how 'very' far the Lord has brought her.

"When I finally accepted that Sean was dying, it was as if half of me was dying. We had been high-school sweethearts. We married in college. He represented all of my dreams. He was a lawyer. I was homemaker and we had the perfect little girl.

"He was diagnosed with throat cancer just as he was about to start a private practice," she recalled. "In the instant I viewed the X-ray with him in the doctor's office, I lost the innocence I cherished. I was no longer the submissive, small-town lawyer's wife. I was a woman with a dying husband.

"Back then I knew nothing about the household, bills or the bank account. I did not know how to drive a car or write a check," she admitted.

"During his 10 month illness, I had to walk through the steps of what it would take for me to live on my own. Gradually, I began to realize I had to separate from him. He was dying and I was living. I did not want to, but I had to.

"Being a young widow is difficult," Maya explained. "My friends misunderstood me most of the time. They had their notion of how I should grieve. But grief wasn't my only battleground. A new person was emerging from within and I did not know what to do with her.

"I first discovered that I am attractive after my husband died. I wanted to be noticed. My friends reacted negatively because I was no longer the quiet, shy person they knew. I started dating soon, four months after Sean's death. My friends did not like that either," she said.

Church acceptance was conditional

Instead of the church being a place of healing, Maya found that acceptance as a widow had definite strings attached.

"The church was very supportive during my husband's illness and death, as long as I was Kate's mommy or Sean's widow. But the emerging single woman refused to stay hidden. I did not know what to do with my sexuality. And the church didn't either.

I did not get the answers I needed from the church. I began asking my pastor questions about singles' sexuality. I wanted him to give me answers, advice, and Bible verses which applied to me as a widow. I needed to know what to do with the sexual being inside me," she said. "My questions and my persistence just made him nervous. I never got any answers about Christian widowhood, just scorn for insisting that sex was an issue. I felt lonely in the church," she said, "and I wondered where did I fit in?"

Though she felt alienated from her church, the new Maya dug deeply within and discovered a closer relationship with Jesus. In her case, the relationship with Christ led to a call to the ordained ministry. Maya's faith has grown and matured much over 15 years. Today she is able to look back on the situation and see God in the midst of everything.

"My spirituality was my survival. I didn't want to be alone, so I went looking for Jesus. When I found him right inside me I was overjoyed. I believed I had been blessed with a great husband and a beautiful daughter. The tragedy of Sean's death was just one part of my story, there has been more, and there is still more to come."

Doris: Tears for healing

Doris my prayer partner is a widow. We met at a singles conference 5 years ago, and we've been praying together ever since then. At 41, she works as a cosmetologist. Although we pray together by phone every Sunday morning, rarely does she talk about her life as a widow. She's always active and cheerful, focusing more on the joys of her life. I sometimes forget that she is still mourning the death of her husband. One Sunday morning, Doris reminded me that she was a widow, saying, "Today is the third anniversary of Carl's death. Pray for me." This simple request gave me a glimpse of her world of quiet sorrow.

"I was married to Carl for eight years," Doris reflected. "He was a strong, robust man, who never showed any signs of illness. Then one day, with no warning, an aneurism killed him.

"Spiritually I knew something was wrong. We had a real connection," she said. "We were so close that he would even have sympathetic P.M.S. (premenstrual syndrome) with me every month.

"At 9:30 a.m. on the day he died, I felt like I was falling off something, even though I was sitting in my chair at the salon. I felt terrible. That feeling was him dying."

Doris's husband died at their home as he dressed for work. He was discovered by his father, who called Doris. Upon her arrival at home, she met police who had dubbed the house a "crimescene," and interrogated her as to her whereabouts. She became a suspect in her own husband's death.

She watched as the paramedics put Carl's body on a stretcher, pulled the sheets over his face and wheeled him to an ambulance.

"My biggest mistake was suppressing the pain, trying to be the perfect, composed widow," she said. "I had it in my head that I was supposed to be a strong woman and not show any emotion.

"But I couldn't bottle it up too long," she continued. "Once I admitted how I was feeling, the Lord ministered to my wounds. I learned the hard way that God's greatest gift of healing is tears to wash away all the pain. When I finally wept, I felt cleansed. I felt a newness of being healed again."

Widowed woman, put the tragedy of your spouse's death behind you. You now face the promises from God of your single splendor. You can experience joy, laughter, and pleasant tomorrows. God is not through blessing you. The widows in this chapter know your suffering, heartache, loneliness. It is a struggle to rise above it, but it can be done with God.

Questions

1. What activities and events bring you joy and lessen the pain of your spouses' death?
2. How can your friends and family best be of assistance to you as you walk toward an empowered life?

Exercise

List 5 of your goals. Schedule each one and accomplish within a year.

Prayer

Pray this prayer every time you think of your spouse for 7 days.

Dear God,
I miss ________________.
I've cried enough tears to fill an ocean.
I want to stop crying and begin to live now.
Help me to cherish his memories, but not be held prisoner by them.
Grant me the strength to accept my singleness.
Bring joy to me.
Strengthen me as I chart new waters.
Allow me to see clearly the blessings that You have in store.
Thank you for my life.
Thy will be done.
Amen.

Principle Six

Single mothers, your children will inherit your power.

YOUNGSTERS WITH A WEALTH OF SELF-ESTEEM AND SELF-LOVE ARE rich beyond imagination. This wealth can be given to children by their parents. Empowered single mothers can rear children who are not ashamed of their mother's singleness.

Single mothers and their children are teams. Their empowerment is interdependent and has its genesis in a cycle of love built on God. The cycle starts with an empowered Christian mother who loves God first, herself second and her children third. The cycle completes itself with children who love God first, themselves second, and their mother third. As long as God is in the center of the team, they can endure the trials of life. Renita learned this lesson when all seemed lost in her life.

Renita: The storm subsided

It took them five years, but finally, Renita and her daughter Rachel recovered from the trauma of divorce. The bitter ending of the marriage had affected both of them drastically. It had been a trial, but they were singing God's praise anyhow.

To celebrate, the two hosted a "house blessing" ceremony in their brand new condominium. A spirit of gratitude filled the air as friends looked back on how far God had brought Renita and Rachel.

Everyone at church knew how the two suffered. We all pitched in with bags of groceries, clothes, and sometimes cash, when the mother and daughter were in danger of becoming homeless. After the divorce Renita's ex-husband, a surgeon, had kept everything in accordance with the prenuptial agreement that Renita had signed. In one day, she and Rachel moved from a Tudor estate on "doctor's row" to a one-bedroom efficiency apartment on the wrong side of the tracks.

What really made her forfeit her life of luxury, was Renita's refusal to let her child to grow up in a home where she believed the marriage was artificial and harmony was a sham.

"I figured out I could suffer by myself," she said. "I didn't need a husband, no matter how rich he was, if he made my life miserable."

Renita's devotion to self and daughter sustained them. Initially she questioned her ability to shoulder the responsibility of parenting alone and sometimes felt guilty for taking her teenager away from the comforts she enjoyed as a wealthy "doctor's daughter."

"My daughter watches me," she continued. "A mother is her daughter's first and most important role model. If she sees me taking abuse, how will that affect her mind?

"The financial strain is intense. Rachel was in high school when the marriage ended," Renita said. "She needed and wanted things I simply could not afford. But she learned to appreciate the things which I could give: faith, love and support."

Renita and Rachel illustrate the teamwork necessary for empowered single mothers and their children. Your coping style is also crucial for the team. Your faith keeps you and your children confident during tribulation. The best advice for rearing children solo may very well be given by airline stewards just before the plane takes off. They say, "First adjust the oxygen mask over your face then adjust the mask on your child's face." Translation- your child will be O.K. if you are O.K.

Tales from the tightrope

Single mothering is like a tightrope you walk while carrying the weight of the world on your shoulders before a tremendous audience. Some of the spectators are rooting for you to make it. Others want you to fall. Either way, though the audience is little help. You have to believe in yourself.

On the tightrope high levels of self-esteem and self-love will provide balance. Accepting your single parenthood will keep you walking. And strong faith in God will let you strut, and even smile from the rope.

Three common complications are potential hazards to successful single mothering: loss of self, guilt at not being able to be all things for your children, and a tendency sometimes to overindulge the children.

Some single moms hurt themselves because they are consumed with their children. This model of parenting unintentionally teaches the children to deny themselves at all costs for the ones they love. This model is unhealthy living and a destroyer of genuine self-love.

It was obvious that Tina had lost something from the way she reacted during a recent single mother's workshop that emphasized good parenting without neglecting oneself. Tina fired at the facilitator, and was never satisfied with the answers. After the fourth round of questions, tears came to her eyes as she moaned. "I want to do things for myself, but I can't," Tina cried. "I am so busy with my children that I have put my needs on the back burner. I can't function any other way.

"I don't dare pamper myself because my kids may go lacking. I don't even know who I am anymore," she said.

Newly divorced, Tina, 25, was terrified of the responsibility for two preschool children. Her parents had not supported her choice to divorce. She moved to a different city to escape their disdain. The distance from home, coupled with the emotional and financial transitions, soon took their toll on her.

By seizing the power of God in her life, Tina could counter her parent's criticism with loving, self-determination, and overcome her tendency to deny herself pleasure.

Taryn: The "sin" of single parenting

Taryn had always been taught that bearing children out of wedlock was sinful. The 22-year-old, often smugly denounced other single women with children, declaring it would never happen to her. But one night she and her boyfriend failed to take proper contraceptive precautions and she became pregnant. Thrust into the role she despised, Taryn felt that both she and her unborn child were doomed. By the time he was four, her son had developed serious emotional problems.

"My son won't behave. I discipline him, spank him and talk to him. I am convinced I am the problem," she confessed one day.

"He is acting up because I am by myself. If I had been able to marry his father, I know my son would be happy and well adjusted," she said.

Taryn mistakenly believed that her family problems simply would vanish if she were married to her child's father. But that is not necessarily so; in fact, it may be a blessing in disguise. Men who shirk their parental responsibilities just because they don't live with the child are not likely to be better live-in parents.

Also Taryn hates her single status and has passed her attitude on to her son. He probably has behavioral problems because his home is unsettled and unhappy. Taryn could improve life for both her and her child if she could learn to use God's power to accept her status, and approach parenting without guilt and shame.

Lillie: Lived to regret it

At a Wednesday evening Bible study session, the scripture focused on Proverbs 22:6, which reads;

"Train up a child in the way that he should go and when he is old, the child will not depart from it."

Lillie, a 65-year-old retiree, read the passage aloud and shook her head in disgust. She was livid and needed to vent her anger. The Bible study class became her forum.

"My sons just won't grow up," she said. "I devoted my life to them when they were boys. Once they became men, I expected their devotion to me, but I get nothing."

Lillie's husband died long ago leaving her to raise her three sons alone. Although the sons were chronologically adults, emotionally they were still boys. While they were growing up she was quite proud of her mothering skills. She loved her boys deeply and did everything in her power to shower them with whatever they requested. The gift giving was Lillie's attempt to compensate for the boy's deceased father.

Lillie prayed that cars, clothes and trinkets had filled her sons' emptiness. In reality, the boys came to expect their mother to meet all needs and desires. To this day the three grown men depend on their mother like toddlers.

Lillie had been a single mother for decades. She parented as best she knew. However, there was more that she needed to do. Changes must be made. Lillie must stop meeting her sons' demands. With God's help she could redirect her parental love to include her sons in a teamwork arrangement that was built on mutual concern. The men need to stand on their feet. And Lillie needs to get them off her lap.

Hagar: Faith role model

Single mothers in the Bible are often depicted seeking divine healing or help for their children. One such mother was Hagar, the Hebrew slave, found in the book of Genesis, chapters 16 and 20. After being cast out by Abraham and Sarah, Hagar's life was in turmoil. She and her young son, Ishmael were homeless, banished into the wilderness with only a loaf of bread and a jug of water. The water and bread were consumed quickly and the duo panicked. At this point, say the scriptures, "God heard the voice of the lad," and rescued the single parent and child from certain disaster.

I believe Hagar knew God would rescue her and Ishmael, because God had rescued her before. Her faith in God was real. Her son benefited by his mother's demonstration of faith. In effect, he was strengthened by her strength. She was his faith role model. In the same way you are your childrens' role model for faith.

By your actions you can ensure that they believe they are worthy, loved, and whole. Your children must be clear on the reality that the number of parents they live with does not determine their worth.

Below I've listed additional ways of being a faith role model for your children. Remember your faith shows in all areas of your life.

• Become prayer partners with your children. Spend time together reading the Bible. Set aside time daily or weekly for family devotion.

• Men are our co-creations, and should be respected. In the presence of your child, do not denounce men in general, or the childrens' father in particular. Negative seeds planted in young minds may program the girls to distrust men and encourage the boys to emulate those you talk about the most.

• Present a balanced view of marriage. While marriage is not a perfect institution, your children deserve the chance to explore it, if they choose. Help your child experience their's or other people's marriages without your negative baggage.

• If you choose to date, do so from the position of strength and not weakness. Your children will learn from your dating habits. If they sense self-hate or desperation, they may mimic you in their relationships.

• Prepare for jealous children, if you date. It is only natural for your children, especially if they are young, to be curious and even resentful of the new man in your life. Give them continuous assurances of your love.

• If you are sexually active, be aware that your habits are observed by your children. It is disrespectful to your children to keep a circuit of men flowing in and out of the house and your bedroom.

• Take a break from your children. Go to a movie or to dinner with friends or alone for a change of pace and peace of mind. Your children also can use the time apart from you.

Martie: She was never alone

The death of a child is the most painful experience a mother can ever know. If left untreated, the venomous pain poisons everything around it. Martie was an empowered single mother who conquered adversities because she knew God was always with her.

I bumped into Martie, an old friend, at the grocery store. She looked well. Her face even radiated with happiness. I asked about her family, and received an answer I never anticipated.

"My oldest son died of AIDS two years ago, my husband died two weeks after that, then my youngest son committed suicide," she said bluntly.

Instinctively, I grabbed and hugged her wondering to myself, "How could she bear all that suffering?"

Martie heard my mumbled question and responded with a smile,

"Well, did you expect me to lay down and die? I've got to keep on living."

Martie was carrying three identities better than some women carry one. She was a widow, a single mom and the mother of two deceased sons all at once. Other women fall apart at such tragedies. They check out of life, overwhelmed by the deaths.

There was something different about her that set her apart from other women. The difference was that Martie refused to be alone. She sought God's presence and maintained it.

When the eldest son died she knew God was there to hold her up. When her husband died, she knew God was there. When her younger son died, she knew God was present too.

"I saw my sons born. I took care of them. And I watched them die," she said softly. "The same God that sustained me when my sons's were teething and I was up with them at 3:00 a.m, is the same God who kept me going when I had to bury them. God really does all those things we believe in."

The empowered single Christian mother knows that she has God on her side no matter how bleak her circumstance may be. It is only her confidence in God that keeps her and her family together. The single moms in this chapter have weathered fierce storms. Most of them are still in tact because they did not walk it alone with their children. God was in the midst of them.

Questions

1. What do you think your children are learning about Jesus from the way you live your life?

2. What do you think your children are learning about singleness from the way you live your life?

Exercise

List 10 of the ways God empowers your family can be happy, whole and productive. Share those ways with your children.

Prayer

Pray this prayer over your first meal of the day for 7 days.

Dear God,
Help me to parent.
Allow my children to see You in me.
Give me the skills and faith that I need to rear my family Your way.
Bring us closer together.
Endow each of us with belief.
Shield us from hardships.
Empower us to appreciate You in our midst.
Amen.

Principle Seven

**Men's love is optional;
Jesus' love is promised.**

JUST LIKE WHIPPED CREAM ON AN ICE CREAM SUNDAE, YOUR relationships with men are optional. What is essential is your bond with Jesus Christ. All other male-related connections hinge on Him.

This is not male-bashing or shrill hysterics. It is good common sense for millions of single women who otherwise would beat their heads against walls because they lack romantic involvement. The good news is they have a choice.

Empowered single women of faith understand that a romantic relationship with a man is not essential to their survival. They are not anti-men, or anti-relationships. They understand that their God-given power enables them to appreciate men, without obsessing about them.

Admittedly, women do not control society, but women must learn to control themselves. When you are in charge of yourself, things don't just happen to you: you speak up, and out, and gain varying degrees of authority. Here's how one woman came to this revelation.

Donna: Trashing the myth of requirement

Donna was man-crazy. She collected men like some people collect matchbooks. She picked them up wherever she went, and was only able to enjoy them for a moment. Once her interest in a man dissipated, she tossed him aside.

"I need a steady flow of them coming in and out of my life or I feel miserable. When I am "in-between" men, I am at my worst," Donna said. "They make me feel valuable whether I know them well or barely remember their names. Their presence makes me a woman. I can't be one without them."

Other women, who like Donna, believe they must have a man in their lives, usually say things like, "I'd feel so much better if I was in a relationship." "Who will take care of me if I don't have a boyfriend?" "A woman without a man is not whole."

These women do not realize other options exist. They are what I call "living limitations" because they are locked into no-win situations that diminish God's power in them. If they have boyfriends, the women are too dependent and their romantic relationship are lopsided. If they do not have steady beaus, the women waste time longing for someone to make them happy while making themselves as well as those around them miserable.

Sadly, these thoughts are too common; many women are addicted to men. It is an obsession with origins in erroneous biblical beliefs of female inferiority. For example, in 1 Timothy 2: 9-15 Paul implies that women gain importance through their men. This sexist Pauline thinking became social and church law and is responsible for centuries of oppression of women.

Jesus never placed women in less valued or less powerful roles than men. He affirmed women and demonstrated throughout his life that women are of equal value. Jesus' behavior shocked many. The disciples were surprised to find Jesus "talking" to a woman in John 4:27.

Also Jesus undoubtedly shocked others when he applauded the boldness of the woman who anointed him with perfume. So important were her actions that in Mark 14:9 Jesus proclaimed:

"...wherever the gospel is preached in the wide world, that also which this woman has done shall be spoken of in memory of her."

Jade: Men were answers to her prayers

When it came to men, Jade was rash and reckless. Sitting in Sunday morning worship service, she bowed her head to pray that her "savior" would enter her life. But she wasn't seeking comfort from Jesus; she wanted a man to save her.

One Sunday when a handsome man walked into the sanctuary, Jade whispered "Hallelujah! my prayers have been answered."

Before he could sit in the pew, she determined him invaluable to her life. She had to have him. Zeroing in on her prey, she cast a series of "I-want-you-to-notice-me," looks in his direction.

After the service she elbowed her way through a throng of predatory women and plunged into a sexually suggestive conversation with him. So clear were her motives that she may as well have worn a neon badge reading "I am desperate, have pity on me."

The single woman who maintains God's power in her life is not a clingy, dependent woman.

In the beginning, God created man and woman. The order in which we were made is not as important as God's original intent, which was a peaceful co-existence between women and men. Consider men co-creations; women and men were both created in the image of God. One gender is not superior or more valuable than the other.

Peace and happiness are possible in female/male relationships under two conditions: men must accept that they do not control women, and women must accept that they do not control men.

The peaceful co-existence between women and men is disturbed by addictive behavior. An addiction to men pushes aside the will of God. Addictions make Christian women blind to what God may really be offering them. Instead of romance right now, the blessing may be a job promotion, time with your children, the opportunity to gain more education, or just peace of mind.

Women who are addicted to men do not fully trust God. They put men in God's role. Their faith in God and desire for men become interchanged. I once heard a single woman joke "I agree with Jesus when he said "If any man will come after me — let him!" Humor aside, addiction to men is a precarious predicament.

There are both good reasons and bad reasons to have a steady man in your life. If you love yourself and enjoy men as additions to your already-pleasant existence, then you can value your man as you value yourself. That makes for a good relationship. But if you do not love yourself, and feel happy only when you are involved with a man, then you cannot bring emotional health and wholeness to any romantic relationship.

The well-managed relationship

The empowered single woman "manages" her relationships with men to her benefit. She treats her male partners as co-creations and, therefore, does not feel victimized in her dealings with them. As much as possible, she determines how she is perceived and is treated by the men in her life.

Women relate most closely with men in four ways: in the family, in platonic friendships, with male mentors, pastors or spiritual leaders, and in romantic relationships. Those relationships will be explored in Principle nine.

Men as friends

Friendships with men are the most satisfying when they are managed properly. Platonic relationships, based on common interests and traits, are usually relationships where men and women are equals. However, your friend is not a substitute for a husband or a father for your children. He cannot be your boyfriend. He has a life of his own. Don't ruin the relationship by smothering him.

Ken and Belinda had been inseparable, since high school. They had all of their classes together and both played clarinets in the marching band. They were so close that they shared the intimate details of dates with each other.

As the buddies aged, fun soon left the relationship. Belinda became fixated on marriage, and became obsessed with finding someone. Ken received the brunt of her unmarried rage.

When Ken met the woman he would ultimately marry, he expected joy and support from Belinda, but she criticized his fiancee', and finally forced Ken to choose between them. Belinda was threatened with Ken's attraction to another woman because Ken was all she had.

The managed platonic relationship begins by treating your friend the way you'd like to be treated. There should be equal give and take in this relationship. Don't make him your emotional dumping ground or punching bag.

Conversely, when he is emotionally down, don't jump in the hole with him. Throw him a rope - your sincere concern. Help him out with prayer.

Men in the family

A close-knit family is an ideal place of nurture for single women. The support network can be marvelous. However, if your father, brothers, uncles, and other male relatives are domineering, oppressive, or abnormally attentive, home can be hell.

Lane and her father had always enjoyed a close relationship. Lane is what is commonly known as a "daddy's girl." Her dad was a widower and Lane was an only child. Even before her mother died, she and her dad were together often.

However, Lane is no longer a girl. She is a 27-year-old woman, with a college degree, a good paying job and a car. She longs for her independence, but is unable to convince her father that she is an adult.

"Daddy won't let me move into an apartment because, he says, 'it's too dangerous for me to live alone'," she complained bitterly. "I don't have many women friends because daddy believes 'so many young people today are out of control.' And I never date because of my dad," she continued. "He constantly tells me, 'you just can't be too sure these days. A guy may look like he's nice, but he may be an axe murderer.'"

Despite the emotional and physical constraints of her father, Lane did realize that as an adult, she had the right to live her own life apart from dear ol' dad. To accomplish this she will have to take a firm, probably painful stance against her father's wishes, and move out of his house and into her own apartment. She should not sever their relationship, just redirect it away from his control over her, and toward a balanced partnership with her dad. This way each person can lead and control their separate lives.

These suggested steps for Lane illustrate one example of the well-managed family relationship. It is a relationship built on independence among the family members and not control over the other. Single women must believe in themselves enough to protect and nurture their singleness, rather than letting it be directed by someone else. The men in your family will come to respect the independent, empowered you, if you stand up for yourself and apart from them. This act defines you as a strong, independent single woman.

Managing relationships with your pastor

"My pastor is a man of God; how much power can I exercise in our relationship?" you ask. The answer is: a lot.

Your relationship with a male pastor can be spiritually rewarding. He has the training and experience to open your eyes to vital faith insights. However, a pastor is also human, and humans make mistakes. A growing number of single women are realizing their need to manage their relationships with their pastors due to the tremendous publicity surrounding clergy sexual abuse scandals. Katrina realized this too late.

Katrina was having problems adjusting to the city. She'd moved here 13 months ago and still had no friends. She considered the pastor a dependable anchor. She did not really know him, but she believed she could trust him because he preached so well and had written her a sincere welcome letter when she joined the church.

She approached him one Sunday after services and asked if he would counsel her. Pastor Jones, a 50-ish, man with graying temples, replied, "By all means I'll counsel you as soon as possible."

A few days later, when Katrina arrived in the pastor's study, his formal tone was replaced by a disturbing familiarity. "Come on in and have a seat, baby," he said, smiling. He motioned her to the couch in the corner of his office. She sat on the left cushion, he sat so close beside her that she saw the hairs on his chest peeking through the shirt he'd loosened.

Katrina tried to mask her misgivings, by keeping her voice level and her eyes straight ahead. Instead of offering her advice on adjusting to the city, Pastor Jones started asking inappropriate questions about who she was dating, what she did on dates, and her sexual preferences.

Katrina wanted to slap his face, but she had been taught to respect ministers. So she turned her anger at him on herself. She left the "counseling" session feeling more frustrated and more alienated than ever. Pastor Jones had victimized Katrina by his sexual advances. She felt even more isolated and alone because of the shame and humiliation his actions caused.

The single woman can best manage her relationship with her pastor by creating a rapport with him in which she can speak without fear. A mutual respect is required along with clear, mutual expectations. Never accept inappropriate behavior or remarks from him. A pastor at his or her best can help you discover the power of God to improve your life and further the kingdom of God. He should affirm you as a single woman, not make you feel guilty or inferior. He shouldn't take advantage of your vulnerability.

Managing your relationship with Jesus

The best managed relationship with Jesus centers on your spiritual life. If you can build a spiritual alliance with Jesus, you will bring an ever-flowing stream of inspiration, joy and hope into your life. A spiritual relationship with Jesus is vital because it serves as the foundation for your life. The decision to relate to Jesus determines your success as an empowered single Christian woman for three reasons. Obviously, you can't be a Christian without Jesus Christ. His life, death and resurrection are the basis for Christianity.

Secondly, Jesus was single. Your concept of singleness should in part be strengthened by his full and productive life. Jesus didn't wait around for marriage to propel himself into action. He went into the world just as he was.

Thirdly, Jesus makes you an effective woman because you know he cares for you. Throughout the New Testament Jesus has an impressive record of helping and empowering women. Jesus maintained a personal attitude toward women that was affirming and uplifting. The empowered woman of faith knows that the love of Jesus in her life can remove the obstacles before her and enable her to do much.

One biblical account of Jesus' concern for women is found in Luke 9: 43-47. There we learn of an unnamed woman who had suffered with a hemorrhage for 12 years. No one had been able to help her. She went to Jesus for healing. So strong was her confidence in him that all she did was grab the hem of his coat. Instantly the bleeding stopped.

Jesus felt power leave his body. He looked down and saw the woman cowering at his side. She explained her situation and how he had healed her. Jesus responded;

"Daughter, your faith has made you well - go in peace."

Clearly there is no way of knowing whether this unnamed woman was single or not. What is important is that she had a spiritual relationship with Jesus which assured her that she could be healed by contact with him.

You need the same conviction. To enter a spiritual relationship, or maintain an existing one, requires commitment and dedication. As with the men in our lives, this relationship requires time and energy also. There are several key elements to your relationship management with Jesus.

Prayer. Daily prayer is a must. Prayer is intentional time spent in conversation with God. You do not need to produce flowing invocations. Rather frequent petitions to God during your day will add ease and confidence to encounters and events. Nothing is too large or too small to pray about. Present all facets of your life to the Lord in prayer, and eventually you will notice a positive difference. God will become a part of all you do.

Meditation. Meditation is the practice of centering your mind on positive thoughts. You may chose to focus on an uplifting account of Jesus affirming women in the New Testament, such as the aforementioned story of the woman with the hemorrhage in Luke 9: 43-47, or the woman who anointed Jesus in Mark 14: 2-9, or the band of women who traveled with Jesus and the male disciples, and functioned as female disciples in Luke 8: 1-3. As you read these accounts, and begin to meditate, focus on the reality that Jesus affirmed those women and the same is in store for you.

Bible study. A spiritual relationship with Jesus is also strengthened by a basic knowledge of Christianity. This can be attained by reading the Bible. Purchase a translation of the Bible that you can easily understand, and read it from cover to cover. It is not enough to hear others talk to you about Jesus, you must learn about Him for yourself.

Public worship. You can also manage your relationship with Jesus by regularly attending worship services at the church of your choice.

There is a high probability that your spirituality will be strengthened if you include a weekly Christian fellowship. Singing hymns, praying and hearing sermons in a congregational setting is enhancing and empowering.

Witnessing. The final management technique I'd suggest requires boldness. Your spiritual relationship with Jesus should not be a secret. You should tell others how you manage it and how it benefits you. Other people, especially single women need to hear how Jesus can come into a life and make a positive difference.

That's what Devin does and she is a blessing to everyone that she encounters. Devin is a 50-year-old widow with a tragic past. Rather than mope, she has managed her relationship with Jesus to create a joyous life that is full of hope. She always shares with others the power of God in her life. On Sundays, she mills about the church before services spreading sunshine.

"Let me tell you what the Lord has done for me this week," Devin said to a group of women as she began to spread her good news. After she shared her triumphs in the Lord she ended the conversation by telling them, "I know that if God blessed me, God will bless you too."

Empowered single women who are managing their relationships with men are living fulfilling and healthy lives. No longer are they victimized. They've recognized that their relationships with the Lord empower them to stop being door mats. The women in this chapter show us that it is not always easy or pleasant to take the reins of control, but it is so, so necessary.

Questions

1.What type of response do you think Jesus' affirming actions toward women received from the society of his time?

2. What area of your life needs relationship management the most?

Exercise

List 10 reasons why you are valuable to Christ.

Prayer

Pray this prayer when you think about the men in your life.

Dear God,
The power to control my relationships is a new and exciting gift.
I need You in the midst of this gift keeping me balanced and focused.
Help me to make wise and compassionate decisions.
Help me to value myself so much that I am intolerant of abuse.
When I feel helpless remind me of Your presence.
I've put my total trust in You.
Amen.

Principle Eight

Dating? Meet "The Man," then meet the man.

NEITHER CLOTHES, HAIRSTYLE NOR FRESH BREATH DETERMINE WHETHER a date with a man succeeds or fails. Prayer is the secret weapon for the socially active, empowered single woman of faith. Armed with prayer, she knows nothing will happen on the date that she and God cannot handle. Therefore, make sure you meet Jesus in prayer before you meet your date. This is how Deborah handles dating.

Deborah: Prayer prepares her

Deborah is a single mom who uses God's gift of empowerment at all times, especially when she dates. Deborah has four children and would like to remarry some day. She dates about twice a month. She would like to get out more, but it's a hassle to shuttle the kids to her mother's home, cleanup the apartment, and transform herself from hard-working single mom, into a show-stopping Ms. Right.

After 10 years of marriage Deborah was unsure of the rules for dating in the 90s. On her first outing she was anxious about the man she was going out with. The women at the restaurant where she is a waitress had introduced him to Deborah. According to her co-workers, he was a "good catch."

Questions whizzed through her head as she raced against the clock to prepare for a 7:30 movie and dinner date. Despite the questions and her nervousness, Deborah was confident all things would work together for the good. She squeezed into the suede pumps that cost half of her waitress's paycheck, zipped up the silk dress she had borrowed from a girlfriend, spritzed on cologne guaranteed to make him remember her name, and waited for a knock at the door.

As she waited, she prayed. Before and after each date Deborah prays. Nothing elaborate. Just enough to celebrate God, who is in control and whose will must be done. Her prayers go something like this:

Dear God,
I am nervous— I don't know anything about this guy.
But You know all about him.
Keep his mind and heart pure and clean.
Mine too.
If he is the one, let me know.
If he's not the one, let me know.
Help me relax. I want to enjoy myself tonight.
Amen

Around midnight Deborah's escort brought her back home. He kissed her on the cheek, and said good night. Once inside, Deborah plopped down on the sofa and kicked off the suede shoes.

"He was nice, but he was not the one," she sighed. "Oh well, you win some, you lose some."

She prayed again as she removed her make-up and went to bed:

Dear God,

Thanks for being there.

I knew You were there when he called me another woman's name by mistake and I did not fly off the handle.

I knew you were there when he conveniently forgot his wallet.

I had to pay for dinner with my credit card.

I don't think he's the one.

But it's in Your hands.

Thy will be done.

Amen.

Do not lean on yourself

Single women who stand on Jesus' foundation develop self-love and self-esteem that enables them to rise above the temptation to lean on their own abilities, rather than God's.

The sobering reality is that dating is a lot like spiritual warfare. There is a battle against the positive power of God in you and the negative powers in our society. Often in our culture women are encouraged to call on anyone *but* God for advice when dating.

Even with faith, the hazards of dating are unavoidable. There is miscommunication, hurt feelings, lies, and game-playing. Women who try and make it without God usually wind up casualties on the dating battle-field. Literally they can fall into three categories; the user, the borrower or the victim.

The user—most commonly known as a "gold digger"—is a woman who chooses men on the basis of what they can do for her, while she offers him little in return.

Theresa was a user and proud of it. "I date those that can help me," she once said. "I can do bad all by myself. I don't need men who are struggling and have little to show for themselves. I want men who have something."

Theresa has always been single, and she plans to continue her lifestyle. "I know how to get what I want from a man, and I don't mind doing it," she continued.

"Right now I only date men who can offer their skills in remodeling my house. I realize these men expect something in return, like sex or whatever else they can get. But it's no big deal because I know what I am getting into. I have clear-cut expectations. I expect to gain."

The user thinks she is in control, but in actuality she relies on the traditionally weak women's means of getting ahead, using her body as a bargaining chip. If users like Theresa would ever claim Christ's power, instead of her own, she'd be shrewd in her relationships with men, not cunning and mercenary. She'd respect men as co-creations, not sugar daddies. On her current path, she is destined to become a bitter, angry woman.

Camille: She borrows men

The borrower is a woman who wastes her singleness by dating married men. She believes that dating married men is ideal for three reasons; they aren't demanding, you know where they are when they aren't with you, and they are stable.

Camille remained in a 3-year tryst with a married father of two. A pastor's daughter, she grew up in a home where right and wrong were clearly delineated. But her black-and-white existance changed after her husband was killed in a car crash. She felt God had abandoned her and began her affair with a married man.

"I know I'm wrong, but I can't help myself," she said. " I don't stop because I feel cheated. I feel the need to strike back at the world.

"I like the excitement of romance in the shadows and the thrill of forbidden love," she said. "We sneak around all the time. We only can see each other at my place. I disguise my voice when I call his office and he does the same when he calls me at work," said Theresa.

"The hardest part of it is that my parents know that I'm dating someone, and they want to meet him. I can't even look them straight in the eyes about the situation. That's what really hurts."

When it comes to another woman's man, the empowered woman has a hands-off policy. Relationships in progress must be respected. The empowered woman also avoids triangles because she is a whole woman who would never settle for a piece of a man's attention.

Biblically, adultery is a serious offense for women and men. The sinfulness of this act is not diminished because you feel cheated by life, or it was his idea. The writer of Proverbs accurately writes that the decitful joy of adultery, leads to hell. In Proverbs 9: 17-18 a midnight rendezvous between forbidden lovers is described:

" 'Stolen water is sweet: and bread eaten in secret is pleasant.' But he does not know that the dead are there. That her guests are from the depth of Sheol."

Jesus offered no flowery words about adultery. He bluntly states in Mark 10: 19:

"You know the commandments, 'Do not murder, Do not commit adultery....' "

He was too good to be true

The victim sees being single as a curse, and she'll do anything to increase her chances of marriage. Victims are self-styled dumping grounds. They accept too much, believe too much, allow too much to happen to them in relationships with men.

June was lonely. She wanted Dan too much. He seemed like her last chance at love and she decided to hang on for what was to become the wildest ride of her life.

When June paid a $300 entrance fee for a dating service on Monday, she had been floored to receive the first call two days later. His name was Dan and it was amazing, he liked to do what she liked to do. His background was similar to hers. Their initial telephone conversation lasted three hours long. Dan said he was eager to meet her, but he was an FBI agent and was out of town a lot. "Please be understanding?" he begged June.

June was more than understanding. Even though Dan called her every day for the following three weeks, their first date didn't come until a month later. During dinner at a romantic restaurant, Dan confessed he'd never met anyone like June before. Overcome with emotion, he proposed. She accepted.

Over dessert, he shared his big secret. He had purchased a plot of land in hopes of building their dream home. Now that she'd agreed to be his wife, they could start the building. Best of all, she could decorate it the way she wanted to. "I trust you," he said.

June took a second job, and began mailing money to Dan to feather their love nest. They continued to talk by phone regularly. He always called, never giving her his home or office phone numbers. "I'm too hard to reach. Let me call you," he urged.

Three months, a bedroom suite and living room sofa later, June finally discovered that she had been conned. She hired a private investigator to find out just who it really was she had agreed to marry. The investigator learned what June already knew but could not admit. "Dan" was an alias and her fiance was not an FBI agent, and of course there was no home.

Empowered women develop a radar to spot lying, conniving men. Empowerment means saying, "Hey I love myself first! I will not tolerate the unexplained absences, the unanswered questions and the promises that never come true. The empowered woman can say goodbye.

Common dating questions

The Christian dating seminars I host are popular, lively events. The attendees come seeking tips for interacting successfully with men, without losing their religion. I'll share the 7 most asked questions.

1. Who should pay for the date?

There is no biblical mandate on footing the bill. Historically men have had all the power and most of the cash. That's why tradition labels them as chief underwriters. Coupled with their buying power, some men assume their money also buys them sexual favors.

Empowered women are beholden to no one and they realize the free ride really never was free. If a man asks you out, let him pay, or offer to split the tab. On subsequent dates, alternate paying, in order to establish an equitable relationship.

2. Can I date more than one guy at a time?

I once saw a bumper-sticker that read, "So many men. So little time." If this describes your dating philosophy, enjoy, but beware. As long as your varied suitors expect no commitment and obligation from you, see as many as you like. However you should realize that the "mass market" approach may not give you time to get to know your dates. In your haste to fill your calendar, you may accidentally overlook the real gem.

3. Is it proper for me to call a man and ask for a date?

Yes. Single Christian women have every right to be assertive and confident in the dating arena. There's no need to sit at home, if you'd rather be out and about in the community. For self-assured women and men it can be exhilarating to swap the traditional female/male, passive/aggressive roles. Select the man you'd like to go out with (making sure as best you can that he is not attached), and map out and entire social event. Then invite him to share your dream date and pick up the tab.

4. Can I date a non-Christian?

Believers and non-believers can enjoy each other's company on a date. It can be fun and educational to learn about another's background. Yet be aware that the differences will likely cause friction in a long-term relationship.

Dating non-Christians is also known as "missionary dating," because you may spend most of the time trying to convert your date to Christianity, or being converted to his. Dating is difficult at best. Obviously you can date whom you chose. My experience leads me to urge you find someone who at least has Jesus in common with you.

5. Should I kiss on the first date?

A quick, dry kiss on the first date can be a signal to him that you'd like to see him again. Deep, passionate kisses physically suggest your desire for a deeper, maybe more physical relationship. In light of this you may want to reserve this intimacy for the later stages of the relationship. If you don't want to see the guy again, don't waste your kisses. Give him a handshake good night.

6. Can I make him marry me?

No. When it comes to marriage, men are like horses that can be led to water, but not made to drink. The more you pressure him, the more he may resist. In such instances, be glad he resists. Nothing is worse than being married to a man who does not want to be married.

7. How long should we date before we marry?

A committed relationship tends to peak after one or two years. By then you will know if he is the one. Over that time you should see him happy, sad, joyous and mad.

There are basic signs that indicate if relationships are solid. Have you met his family? Have you introduced him to yours? Do you two date publicly, or is it a secret?

If you feel you still don't know him well enough after regular dating for a year of two, this is probably a sign that you never will.

You should decide whether to keep investing yourself in the relationship once you determine where it is headed, and if you want to go in that direction with him.

Is he right for me?

Empowered women recognize that they do not assess men by their outer trappings. A late model car, stylish wardrobe and high paying job do not necessarily add up to a man worthy of their time.

Some women have a habit of dating men who are bad for them. They unconsciously gravitate toward destructive men who abuse them, will not commit to them, and constantly lie to them.

Identifying the men you don't want is perhaps more important than looking for those you do want. When you meet a man you think you'd like to know better, answer these questions about him before you become deeply involved.

1. How does he handle anger?
2. What was his childhood like? Was he an abused child?
3. How does he act with children? With pets?
4. What does he think about his mother?
5. What kind of self-esteem does he have?
6. Does he act controlling or possessive of you?
7. Does he have an adequate support system?
8. Is he addicted to alcohol or drugs?
9. Is there a history of mental health problems in his family?
10. Will he communicate his thoughts with you?

If the man you are considering is angry, possessive, drug-addicted or mentally ill, do not see him any more. Another common dating problem is that women, particularly Christian women, want to help everyone they meet. They see a "troubled man," as a project, and want to help him get his life together. Leave the miracle work for Jesus.

Managing romance

Principle 7 taught the value of exhibiting control in all of your relationships with the men, including Jesus. Your ability to control yourself and your surroundings is of the most importance in your romantic relationships. If you decide to enter a romantic relationship walk into it with your eyes open, your brain functioning and your faith in God working overtime.

Love is a gift from God, and when you share it with a man, you can experience an unspeakable bliss. However, love has also been known to make fools of those who dare to enter in.

"I'm in love!" Romona declared, walking into my office. I did not know whether to congratulate her or offer her sympathy. I worried about Romona because I was not sure if she was ready for another relationship. Her husband's suicide was devastating . She felt guilt, embarrassment and isolated. That's a deep hole to climb out of.

She described her relationship with Percel in glowing terms. "We are great together. He understands and accepts me just as I am," she said. "We've been seeing each other for two months and I enjoy him because I enjoy myself. It took me a while to reach this point of self-love, but it makes my love for him possible."

In a well-managed romantic relationship you are not consumed with love to the point that you are putty in his hands. Keep your backbone and remain who you were when you started the relationship. In order to accomplish this monitor yourself for indications that you are changing to please. Occasionally stand back and honestly appraise the relationship. Ask yourself these questions. Is this what I expected? Am I satisfied? Can I do better?

The empowered women of faith date with a calmness. They know that a first date is not necessarily a signal to make wedding plans. Rather they seek to enjoy themselves and the men they are with. They leave the rest to God. They pray before, after, and during the dates, knowing that prayer is more powerful than the most expensive perfume or stylish dress. The women you met in this chapter are all struggling to date with their faith prominently displayed. Jesus gives them the confidence to believe that no matter how the date goes, it will be alright.

Questions

1. What would you pray about before and after a date?
2. Have you ever been a "victim," "user," or "borrower?"

Exercise

List 5 men you know, that you'd like to go on a date with. Select one, and invite him out.

Prayer

Pray this prayer when you accept a date.

Dear God,
Don't let me begin or end a date without You.
I need Your strength with me in a mighty way on those occasions.
My emotions run so high.
I sometimes get so confused.
I forget that I can turn to You and find peace.
In You I find answers to so many questions.
As long as I feel Your presence I am confident.
Amen.

Principle Nine

Single sexuality: choice is power.

SEXUALITY IS A GOOD GIFT FROM GOD. GOD GAVE IT TO YOU. THEREfore you can decide what to do with it. Don't be suckered, cajoled or intimidated into someone else's decisions.

Choice is power. I observe empowered single women wrestling with this power to choose. They make their choices on the basis of their relationship with God. It can be frustrating, and difficult. The choice has always been there. The guts to make the choice from an empowered stance has not.

Traditionally, any bravery women had dissolved into acquiescence as fierce societal inequities and double standards converted sex into the single women's no-win situation. The single woman is "damned if she does have sex," i.e. slandered and condemned. And she is "damned if she does not have sex," i.e. teased and labeled.

Here's one woman's encounter with choice.

Saundra: An usher's dilemma

Saundra's feet began to hurt in those high heels she shouldn't have worn on the Sunday she ushered. So she momentarily slipped out of the sanctuary and headed downstairs to the ladies' lounge for a quick respite. Hurrying through the basement corridor, she saw Ken sipping a cup of coffee in the kitchen. He was the church treasurer, and the man of her dreams. She had prayed for the day when they could have a conversation alone. She decided, that day had come. Saundra forgot all about the ladies' lounge, and made a beeline for Ken. Her feet didn't hurt that bad.

Ken's motions invited her to follow him into a dim kitchen corner for privacy in a public place. Slowly they embraced. Their lips met and their bodies melded into one. There was passion, heat, and fluttering heartbeats.

Between steamy kisses she mused to herself, "The congregation is upstairs singing to the heavens. And down here the church treasurer and head usher are raising hell! Call it lust. Call it lewd. Call it licentiousness. But it feels good."

Ken's hands initially grasped her waist. Ever so slowly they began heading south. She knew what was next. Their corner of the kitchen was adjacent to a dark and spacious pantry. No one would find them there.

Saundra had to make a decision fast. She had choices. She could stop the heated exchange and possibly cause him to lose interest in her. Or she could participate in what could be the best sex of her life and surely secure Ken as "her" man.

Before Saundra was able to decide, another usher nudged her arm and interrupted her sexy daydream. "Hey, wake up, it's time to collect the offering, come on!" the woman scolded.

Readers, if I had a means of polling the outcome of Saundra's fantasy, I believe the verdict would be evenly split. Half would encourage her to explore a sexual relationship with Ken. Perhaps not in the church kitchen pantry, but at a later time. The other half would ask Saundra to pry Ken's hands off her hips, dose herself with cold water, and slow that relationship down to a sexless, hand-holding evening at the church social.

Obviously, sex is an issue that single Christian women disagree on vehemently. From my experience, I've seen singles who practice celibacy, condemn those who are sexually active. And I've seen sexually active singles belittle the sexual celibates. I 've been singed in that crossfire enough times to learn that condemnation of either choice is ineffective. The mistake is attempting to tell women and men what to do with their sex lives. Years ago my style of ministry was preaching damnation to the fornicators and threatening them with the wages of their sins. Luckily it dawned on me, single adults are exactly that - adults. They will do what they want to do, regardless of fiery preaching and threats from hell. That's when the idea of choice came to me. The choice to become sexually active should be a conscious decision, not entered into lightly.

Each woman should stop and count the costs, especially virgins. In order to make an informed, inspired choice, pray about it, read your Bible, and talk with other Christian women. Choice is power.

Have you figured out my stance yet? I advocate the celibate life for single Christian women for lots of reasons beyond, "God will zap you if you do it." My stance was not made in a sterile, virginal bastion of archaic ministry. I know the urge for sexual intimacy is so strong it can curl the hair and the toes. I know sexual pleasure is distinct and rich. I know intercourse with the man you adore can put a smile on your face and a spring in your step, that lingers weeks after the event.

But, I also know that sex outside marriage is problematic. Most women view sex differently than most men. We women take sex seriously. We understand intercourse as an act of genuinely giving ourselves. We are at risk. Therefore, sex is risky.

There is the risk of being abused. Some single women become sexually active because they choose to follow the rhythms of external powers such as temptation and manipulation. They have been tricked into believing that sex equals love, or sex guarantees fidelity from their boyfriends, or sex is the only way to share intimacy with men.

Sex presents health risks through the contraction of a long list of curable, sexually transmitted diseases. The currently incurable diseases such as herpes and the H.I.V. virus are also real dangers to be considered in your choice.

Sexually active women face a societal risk. The double standard rewards men for sexual prowess and condemns women for it. Therefore if a single woman is sexually active in a relationship and her actions become public knowledge, she may be subjected to personal regret, a sullied reputation and guilt, even though her partner was equally as participatory as she.

Jesus and the choice of sex

Most importantly, there are religious risk. Jesus had strong opinions about sex between single persons. He did not seek to harm the involved persons, rather he pointed them away from sexually activity and toward other choices.

In John 8: 3-11, Jesus is challenged by a group of religious leaders to decide the penalty for a woman caught in the act of sex outside of marriage — specifically adultery.

Rather than stoning the accused woman to death, as was the custom, Jesus stooped down and began to write in the dirt with his fingers. Then he offered the following advice for all of her accusers.

"He who is without sin among you, let him be the first to throw a stone at her."

No one knows what Jesus wrote in the dirt, but we assume that the combination of his spoken and written words caused each of the men to leave the scene in silence. Jesus then turned to the woman and said,

"Neither do I condemn you, go your way. From now on sin no more."

I interpret Jesus' words to this biblical woman who apparently chose sex outside marriage, to mean that his forgiveness is offered and changes in choice are expected.

Not only did Jesus offer forgiveness and suggest a change of choice for the sexually active singles, he also suggested a means for curbing the sexual urge. Jesus knew long before psychiatrists discovered it, sex is all in the mind.

In Mark 7: 21, Jesus explained to a group of listeners the connection between our thoughts, and our actions. Then Jesus listed "evil" behavior that begins in the mind. Included on the list is sexual intercourse by unmarried people or "fornication."

This means mind control is vital for the empowered single woman who chooses celibacy. If you believe you can live a fulfilling life that does not include sexual relationships, you can do it. You can be an empowered celibate woman, who lives by God's word and is fueled by God's promises.

Sexual battleground

From my pastoral perspective, the singles' sex scene is often like a battleground. The casualties are numerous and primarily women. Sex hurts sometimes. It is not always engaged in for pleasure. Desperation, loneliness, and debilitating self-hate keep some women jumping in and out of beds, without knowing why.

Sometimes sexually active Christian singles have negative experiences with their sexual choices. In times like those they can benefit from a concerned, compassionate, and contemporary pastor.

Saddly, some pastors like to pretend that sexual activity is not taking place among their church's single population. Singles and sex make them nervous. Unfortunately this naive attitude inflames the situation by causing singles to lean more on the sex and less on the pastor.

Singles want to talk about sex with their ministers in non-threatening, affirming conversations. They want to know what the Bible says about sex and how they can apply those teachings to their lives. Singles want to share their experiences, but they don't want to be tongue-lashed for their openness.

I welcome dialogue with singles about the choices they make. That's why I was happy when Tanya, a woman in my church, called to make an appointment. I had a feeling sex was on her mind, and it was. Tanya and her boyfriend were sexually active in a committed relationship. Both of them had been married before and felt blessed to have found the other. She was understandably proud that their relationship had conquered the hills and valleys of love, and lasted three years.

Although the couple often talked of marriage, there were no formal plans underway. They simply enjoyed each other, and that was enough. In the meantime they felt very comfortable and spiritually sound with the sexual component of their relationship. Yet something brought her to my office to talk about sex. During her visit we talked candidly .

"As long as I am in a committed relationship, sex is alright. Right?" Tanya asked. The tone of her voice indicated she assumed I would agree. Tanya was wrong on both counts.

"Although marriage is not a perfect institution, it is the best relationship for marriage due to its tangible commitment," I said. Tanya came prepared to debate the issue. She countered my statement by offering her impressions of God.

"I don't think God intended for grown people to live without sexual contact," she explained. "Everybody needs touches, hugs and love," she urged. "Surely the rules against sex are for immature children who do not know what they are doing. Adults are mature and responsible."

Tanya was correct to an extent here. Biblical mandates prohibiting sex outside marriage are for children. And we are all *children* of God, regardless of our age. God watches us from the heavens like a mother watches her child playing outside. God wants only the best for us. That's why guidelines exist.

I responded to Tanya by reminding her, "Christianity is a demanding faith, not a cafeteria-style system, where one selects beliefs to match personal preferences, the way one selects a handbag to match a dress."

I understood her difficulty. It is not easy for singles, or anybody else, to adhere to biblical teachings. We live in a world with few rules. Today's popular philosophy proclaims; "if it feels good, then do it." To make these tough decisions, single women who choose celibacy need God to endow them with a strong will and matching chastity belt!

Tanya realized her first two rationales failed to convince me. Then she threw her trump card into the conversation.

"Sex makes me a whole woman," she said.

"Are you one half of a woman without sexually intimacy?," I asked.

"No way," Tanya snapped. "I am a whole woman because I have a man in my life."

Her answers revealed that perhaps Tanya had built her wholeness on what another human could do for her. And empowered woman knows that her wholeness must come from within herself and from God. It should not be derived from someone else, no matter how much the person loves her, what he can do for her or to her. It is dangerous to give anyone that much authority in our lives. If Tanya wants an authentic, empowered womanhood, she will build it on the eternal and divine. All other ground is sinking sand.

Pregnancy clouded the issue

I met Sharmaine at a recent singles seminar and she said needed to come for counseling quick. She had to practically drag Benjamin, her boyfriend, with her for their first session with me. The two had come for premarital counseling, even though they had only been dating six months, and Benjamin had not firmly committed to marriage. The pressing issue was Sharmaine's expanding abdomen.

With each subsequent visit from this pair, it became clearer that Benjamin nor Sharmaine wanted to marry. He offered a host of excuses as to why Sharmaine was not ready for marriage. He refused to consider marriage until she could prove to him, she was ready.

Sharmaine was confused and scared about the entire situation. Although she did not know Ben very well, she felt compelled to marry to him due to the baby that was due soon. She was angry about the stress the pregnancy had caused on their relationship.

"Even though we both had sex, I am bearing the results, the responsibility, and the potential for rearing this child. I wish there was a way things could be more equally distributed," she complained.

These two 30-year-old Christian single adults entered into a sexual relationship to derive pleasure. The unexpected pregnancy fast-forwarded them into plans for a wedding neither of them wanted.

Lola: Sex is my reward

Lola, a 40-year-old widow, works hard as an interior decorator and, as a single mother of four school-age children. In Lola's opinion, sex is her personal reward.

Raising four children alone was difficult, she reasoned. She gave much of herself to the children, but who was taking care of her? Sexual intercourse was the comfort she chose to fill her void. In fact she needed comfort many nights a week. A variety of men spent nights at her home, depending on who she was in the mood for.

Lola did not come in for counseling about her sexual activity. Rather, she was upset that her eldest daughter was following her lead and was now sexually active. Lola couldn't understand the connection between her sexual involvement and her child's interest in sex.

Lola soon realized that as a single parent, her sexual choices impacted her children whether she liked it or not.

Celibacy is hard work

Your body and your faith must be in harmony. Celibacy offers this harmony because it matches your faith with your deeds.

Any endorsement of celibacy as an option for single Christian women of all ages and situations, must also realistically include the difficulties with this lifestyle. Any advocate must truthfully state what celibacy is and is not.

Celibacy is a means of expressing your faith. It most effective when it is understood as a gift from God. Many people begin the life of sexual abstinence by asking God to endow them with the gift of celibacy. They pray that all sexual urges will be removed from their minds and replaced with pure thoughts. Other celibates report that they draw their strength to refrain by meditating on how clean and "unburdened" their souls feel when they abstain from sex.

While celibacy has its benefits, it is not a utopia. It does not guarantee perfect relationships or lead to perfect marriages. Nothing human can ever be perfect. We can only try to strive for God's ideal, which I believe, celibacy is.

Celibacy is not to be entered into when you are angry with the man in your life, and you want to punish him. It is not a tool that makes you appear alluring. Also celibacy is not a reason to become arrogant and pious. That's what happened to a celibate woman I met named Christine.

Christine truly loved the Lord. She was even more enamored with her faith as her steps toward a completely celibate life were strengthened by God. With God's help, she had been transformed from one of the most sexually well-known women around the church, into a woman who lived the life as prescribed by the Bible. The problem was, the more she adhered to the scriptures, the more self-righteous she became.

Christine wore her celibacy like a sheriff's badge. She was determined to enforce God's law in her life and everyone else's. Christine's method was sharp criticism and public put-downs. She would broadcast everyone else's business, thinking that gossip would shame them into conversion.

Her actions demonstrated that celibacy does not make one better than everyone else, rather it is an extra responsibility. Those who choose celibacy are closely watched by those who have not. The onlookers want to see if the celibate is happy, content and able to function without sex. Unfortunately, Christine turned people away from celibacy.

Rather than taking the superwoman approach to sexual restraint. Barbie accepts the trials and tribulations she faces daily. Recently divorced after 7 years of marriage, she confesses that going without sex is like withdrawal from some type of drug.

"I pray everyday without ceasing," she said. "It is so hard to live without sex, when you have been accustomed to it.

"Sometimes I crave a man so bad that I ball up on the floor and cry. I know that sex outside marriage is unacceptable to God. I am struggling with God's word," she said.

"The really hard part is dating," Barbie continued. "Guys I meet, even guys from church, do not want to hear anything about celibacy. Most of them laugh when I bring the topic up. But I am determined to stick with it."

Choice is power, and making the decision can be agonizing. Empowered women make their decisions about sex on the basis of their faith. They pray for the strength to live their beliefs. Ultimately they know the decision and the consequences are between them and God. What this world says is not important.

Questions

1. Why do you think Jesus offered the woman caught in adultery forgiveness?
2. When did you discover you had a choice to make about your sexuality?

Exercise

Give some genuine thought to the celibate life and make a list of 10 things you would enjoy participating in, rather than sex.

Prayer

Pray this prayer at bedtime for 7 days.

Dear God,
I am a sexual being.
You made me this way.
Help me decide what to do with myself.
I can satisfy my sexual needs or give them over to You.
I have choice to make, but I need help.
Sexual temptation is all around me.
It comes in many forms.
I want to do Your will.
Give me the strength.
Amen.

Principle Ten

Sharing power is an obligation.
Lift others as you climb.

EVERYONE MUST KNOW THAT EMPOWERED SINGLE WOMEN ARE HAPPY alone, divorce wounds heal, bereavement pangs lessen, and single parent families succeed. Get on the telephone. Write a letter. Tell somebody. Inform the world. The unempowered women need to hear the life-changing good news, that Jesus loves them just as they are.

Empowered single women understand that the task is clear and uncompromising. With each positive step they take, they must reach out and help another single woman on her journey toward a complete life. Empowerment is an obligation to help others. It is your responsibility to spread the good news that singlehood is not a curse.

Bonnie: From the bottom to the top

My friend Bonnie took her obligation seriously. Years ago, she was the feminization of poverty personified. Today she heads a multi-million dollar life insurance company that she built from scratch. Despite the busy lifestyle of this 48-year-old C.E.O., Bonnie intentionally dedicates time to help women who currently live like she once did, by teaching basic finance courses to women's groups. Bonnie teaches finance because she believes it is an area where women are weakest.

Two decades ago, Bonnie admits she could barely spell the word "finance." Divorced and responsible for her three children, Bonnie had no skills, no education and no money.

"My story has a sad beginning," she said. "I was a poor, divorced woman from a small town. Although I kept my children, I had no means of supporting them. I was miserable.

"One day I got tired of being miserable," Bonnie explained. "That very day I stopped feeling sorry for myself. I realized I could change my situation if I worked hard and believed in myself."

Bonnie reflected back on her moment of change.

"God awakened me and gave me the strength to be a new woman. My faith blossomed the more I relied on the Lord. I found the courage to complete high school and college. I know God was pushing me to excel," she said.

"The more I learned, the more I shared with other women around my neighborhood. I taught one group of single mothers how to establish household budgets. I helped another group of women establish bank accounts. It took years to build my insurance company, and every step of the way I paused long enough to encourage other women," she added.

It is important to note that Bonnie moved from a condition of powerless to powerful, and simultaneously remembered others as she ascended. She illustrates the reality that authentic love for God produces love for others. In fact, the empowered single woman should be uncomfortable knowing that some of her sisters still live in spiritual and emotional dungeons. Her love and concern for other women serves as lights for their pathways.

Miss Sims: Empowerment is contagious

God's spiritual empowerment is contagious. In many instances you can assist others simply by being your confident, courageous self.

When I was a girl, just being in the same room with Miss Sims always boosted my self-esteem a few notches higher. She was a friend of my mother's and visited our home occasionally.

Miss Sims was the only single woman I knew back then. All the other ladies were wives and mothers. But not Miss Sims. She wasn't connected to anybody, and she wasn't shedding any tears about it. She lived her life and enjoyed being who she was.

In retrospect, I now know that Miss Sims affected me deeply. She was my first role model for empowered single womanhood. I was proud in her presence, proud of her, and proud that I knew a woman like her.

She never lectured me about the virtues of remaining single. Her quiet confidence spoke loudly of her contentment. She set my mind on a future that held no limitations or concretized expectations. I knew I could be somebody whether I married or not because she was somebody. She gave me my freedom as a woman to choose what I wanted to be.

Sins of the single

Sin is a word that I use sparingly. It is employed at this point to describe the worst act an empowered single woman can commit; refusing to empower others.

Your power is your blessing. In the words of the old gospel song, your power is "your little light," that needs to shine. Jesus knows you have been empowered, and he expects you to live differently and help others. Jesus' directive from Matthew 5: 16 highlights what he expects from you.

"Let your light shine in such a way that single women may see your good works and glorify your God in heaven."

An empowered woman who refuses to help others is tragic. She is one who selfishly keeps her power locked inside, while single women around her are sinking. Her skills include impeding positive progress, shredding fledgling self-esteem and shoving down women on their way up from life on the their knees.

Why do some women oppress others? Such women do not understand the power of God in their lives. God's power has been misunderstood and misappropriated since the beginning of humanity. Traditionally, men were the primary perpetrators, who kept women in "their place." Now that women have greater access to power, some of them abuse as well.

Jasmine: The oppressor was a woman

There were always confusion when Jasmine was in the vicinity. Arguments and friction with other women seemed to originate with her. Initially, I held high expectations for Jasmine, hoping she would become a spiritual leader of the church's singles' group. Rather than lead, she stifled the other singles.

A painful divorce shattered her emotions. She worked diligently to rebuild her shattered self-esteem, and could have been a source of hope to others suffering from the break-up of their marriages.

Single women of faith share a bond of commonality which creates their community. There is responsibility within this community. The stronger are expected to help the weaker.

Jasmine did not understand she was an important part of the community. Rather, she functioned like an independent island, touching no one. Empowerment was a weapon she used to keep others down and herself up. The possibility exists that this single woman will realize the seriousness of her connection to others. However, she may realize it too late.

Martha and Mary: The ties that bind

Leading women to the empowered life is not always easy. They may resent your interference or ignore your advice. The biblical account of sisters Mary and Martha illustrates the problem and underscores the reasons why you don't stop trying.

According to Luke 10: 38-42, Martha and Mary were two single sisters who saw life very differently. Martha's mind was limited to the household. Mary's mind may originally have been there, but when Jesus dropped by their home for a visit, Mary's thoughts and life were drastically changed.

It was Martha who spotted Jesus and his disciples walking through their small village. Eagerly, she invited them into the home she and Mary shared. She showed Jesus her love with the traditional ways of women; by serving, cleaning and cooking. Mary became so excited by the presence of Jesus that she forgot all about the housework. She sat near him and tried to listen to every word he spoke.

This scenario of the two single women who encounter Jesus teaches us that every woman will experience and react to Jesus differently. Meeting Jesus means we will have to change something about ourselves.

Martha was forced to face radical change. In verse 41 Jesus chastises Martha for her excessive concern with the old ways. Then he urges her to listen and learn his message of empowerment, so that, like Mary, she might be changed.

Jesus told Martha;

"Martha, Martha, you are worried and bothered about so many things; but only a few things are necessary, really only one, for Mary has chosen the good part, which shall not be taken away from her."

Mary and Martha represent empowered and unempowered single women of faith. Martha responded to Jesus the best way she could. I do not condemn her for offering her best. Mary responded by being transformed. She put aside her old self and put on a new self that was focused on Christ and her relationship with him.

Mary's actions are instructive as you execute Principle ten. Three points are prominent.

Don't ask for power, seize it.

Mary did not ask permission to leave the housework and sit with Jesus. She did it. You too, can put aside housework, and take the time to improve your situation.

Live differently and better because you know Jesus.

Mary must have seen in Jesus an escape from a tradition that kept women in limited roles. Your acquaintance with Jesus enables you to see new and improved ways of conducting your life.

The women who need your help the most will fight it the most.

Martha's anger with Mary occurred because Mary dared to change her self-perception, attitude and actions with Jesus' power. The new, empowered you will ruffle feathers. Unempowered women may look at you and become angry with your new style. Maintain your attitude of assistance and keep on being a role model.

Methods of empowerment

In the spirit of Mary who eagerly accepted the power of Jesus in her life, and became an instant role model, consider the suggested methods of empowering others listed below. Chose those that you can accomplish, and get busy.

1. Be an empowered single mentor. Someone needs a guide for living the single life with Christ at the center. Help her through the valleys, you've already crossed. Walk her through the storms with your umbrella of experience.

2. Host a brunch, lunch or dinner at your home for women who are struggling with their singleness. Use the mealtime for sharing survival, and networking skills.

3. Talk candidly with women who are being battered and abused by the men in their lives about ending those relationships. Some women do not know they deserve better treatment.

4. Go to a local women's jail or prison and teach these single power Principles. Many imprisoned women committed crimes to please the men in their lives. They need empowerment to break the cycle of abuse.

5. Befriend a married woman. Some married women feel they are more important than single women, due to the wedding band on their finger. Married women need empowered single women friends to keep their perspectives balanced.

6. Become an empowerment evangelist. Tell every single woman you meet what Christ has done for you and your singleness.

7. Speak honestly to girls about their access to empowerment. As early as possible, they need to know they are powerful and they have choices.

8. Locate men who are not threatened by empowered single women. Encourage them to teach more men that women have a right to power.

9. Teach boys to respect women, and their rights to powerful lives.

10. Offer to led a session on these Principles of empowerment for your Sunday school class or other educational environment.

11. Encourage your pastor to read this book and preach a sermon about an empowered single biblical woman.

12. Start a single woman's support group in your church, school or community.

13. Use holiday gatherings as occasions to help the unempowered women in your family. You can also seek to learn more from those women in your family who already are empowered..

14. Protest the negative images of single women presented by the media. All single women are not sex-crazed, man-hungry neurotics.

15. Gather young single women around empowered single senior citizens to hear their elders speak about their survival.

Empowered single women care about other women. For them empowerment is an obligation of joy. They embrace it with the anticipation of change. The empowerment you possess is the ability to change the character of this society, one woman at a time. Your irrepressible capability to care about others, and help them, comes from God. You can be someone else's blessing right now.

Questions

1. How have single women helped you handle your singleness?
2. How have single women hurt the way you handle your singleness?

Exercise

List your top 5 strengths as a single woman. Consider ways of sharing your strengths with other single women as soon as possible.

Prayer

Pray this prayer as you drive to work, school or run errands for 7 days

Dear God,
Give me an urgent desire to spread the good news.
I have been blessed with Your power in my life.
Help me to be a blessing to other women.
Fill my heart with your joy.
Endow me with boundless energy.
Place Your words into my mouth.
Send me where You want the good news shared.
Strengthen me to handle rejection from my unenlightened sisters.
I can do all things through You.
Amen.

Conclusion

My mission is complete. I've carried around a burning need to speak a word of candor and encouragement to single Christian women for many years. I've heard their cries and sorrows. I've witnessed them achieve and soar.

As I wrote this book I felt like a coach on the sidelines of an athletic field, offering support and guidance to a group of players. Surely the single life is no game. But a strategy is needed if one intends to win. I want single women to win. I want stereotypes, sexism, hopelessness, low self-esteem and self-hate to lose. If you've thought twice about your situation. If you've reevaluated a relationship. If you've read the scriptures anew, then my labor has not been in vain.

Now that you've read this book, pass it on to other single women who need to hear a positive word. Then pass it on to your married friends. They need to understand and appreciate your situation. Also, encourage the men in your life to read this book. It may provide the answer to the popular question, "what do women really want?"

Most of all, understand that empowerment is a lifelong process. As long as there is breath in your body, keep seeking God's power. Christians can never get too much of the Lord.

Order Form Perseverance Press

- ***Single Principles: The Single Woman's Ten Step Guide to Power,*** **Perseverance Press, 1993.**
  116 pages, softcover, $9.95
  These power principles can change your life.

Ordering Information

Name

Address

City | State | Zip

Phone number

Single Principles | $9.95 |
Book title | Price | Quantity

Subtotal

Sales tax (Texas residents only, 8.25%)

Shipping ($2.00 per book)

Total order (check or MO enclosed)

Mail to:
Perseverance Press
6212 Samuell Boulevard, Suite 148
Dallas, TX 75228